Crafty FAMILY IDEAS

SAFETY NOTE

You can involve your kids in making all of these projects and recipes, but be safe when using hot glue, craft/hobby knives, ovens, etc. You know your kids and their ages, so you decide when supervision is needed and when it's better for you to take over the potentially hazardous steps.

© 2021 by Kristin Gambaccini and Fox Chapel Publishing Company, Inc., 903 Square Street, Mount Joy, PA 17552.

Crafty Family Ideas is an original work, first published in 2021 by Fox Chapel Publishing Company, Inc. The patterns contained herein are copyrighted by the author. Readers may make copies of these patterns for personal use. The patterns themselves, however, are not to be duplicated for resale or distribution under any circumstances. Any such copying is a violation of copyright law.

Note: The use of products and trademark names (including but not limited to Band-Aid®, Betty Crocker™, Honey Nut Cheerios™, Pirouette®, Popsicle®, SPAM®, Styrofoam™, Tater Tots™, and Wayfarer®) is for informational purposes only, with no intention of infringement upon those trademarks.

ISBN 978-1-4971-0159-3

Library of Congress Control Number: 2020952966

All photos by the author unless otherwise noted. The following images are credited to Shutterstock.com and their respective creators: cookie cutters (page 4): horiyan; paper cones (page 60): PENpics Studio; school lunch checklist icons (page 157): Volha Shaukavets; Bright Idea icon (throughout): Shutterstock Vector; Project icon (throughout): Panda Vector; Recipe icon (throughout): FishCoolish

To learn more about the other great books from Fox Chapel Publishing, or to find a retailer near you, call toll-free 800-457-9112 or visit us at *www.FoxChapelPublishing.com.*

We are always looking for talented authors. To submit an idea, please send a brief inquiry to acquisitions@foxchapelpublishing.com.

Printed in the United States of America
First printing

Crafty FAMILY IDEAS

Projects to Make, Things to Bake, and Lots of Homemade(ish) Fun

KRISTIN GAMBACCINI

Fox Chapel
PUBLISHING

Contents

Introduction 6
Our Story 8

Chapter 1: Spring Break. 12

Embellished Umbrella 14
Mommy Daddy Nights. 17
Tater Tot Casserole 18
Pet Silhouette. 20
Eggshell Planting 25
Dog Treats 26
Tin Can Art Storage. 28
Art Display. 31
No-Bake Energy Balls 32
Rainbow Centerpiece. 34
Drinking Glass Flower Vase 37
Carrot Cake 38
Sidewalk Popsicle Chalk 40
Popsicle Stick Numbers 45
Chocolate Chip Oatmeal Banana Bars . . . 46

Chapter 2: Kicking Off a Creative Summer 50

Bubblegum Machine 52
Vacation Travel 57
Caramel Corn Snack 58
Ice Cream Cone Garland 60
Birthday Party Craft 65
Homemade(ish) Dr. Cake 66
Book Pouch 68
Lazy Susan Herb Planter 72
Homemade Bug Spray. 75
Sunflower Wreath 76
S'mores Station 81
S'more S'mores. 82

Chapter 3: Fall-ing Back into Routine 86

Candy Apples (Nonedible) 88

Packed Lunches 91

Homemade Applesauce 92

Jack-o'-Lantern Candy Holder 94

Pumpkin Saver 97

Dinner in a Pumpkin. 98

Candy Corn Buttons 100

Fancy Crust 105

All-Butter Piecrust 106

Perfectly Perfect Apple Pie. 108

Pumpkin Pie Garland 110

Game Day 115

Thanksgiving Casserole. 116

Homemade Potpourri 118

Chapter 4: Crushing the Winter Doldrums . . . 122

Cozy Coaster 124

Cup Tray 127

Mug Sweater. 128

Gingie Cookie Kids & Easiest Royal
Icing Ever 132

Gingie Kids (Nonedible) Ornaments 134

Hot Cocoa Snowman 136

Seek-and-Find Activity Balls 139

Grinch Cookies 140

Cookie Bag. 142

Gift Wrap Matters 147

Best Ever Sugar Cookies 148

Feather Tree 150

Silver Storage 153

Celebration Chocolate Chip Cookies. . . . 154

Templates. 156

About the Author 158

Acknowledgments 158

Praise for This Book 159

Index 160

Introduction

People often ask me what my secret is for raising eight children. In all these years, I've picked up plenty of tips and tricks to keep the kids occupied, make our home functional and beautiful, and create easy and yummy recipes that are a treat for everyone—all while staying somewhat sane and not spending an arm and a leg. And I want to share these tips (which really work!) with you in the hopes that you'll get as much joy and love out of my family's crazy shenanigans as I have.

This book is full of fun and inexpensive (or even free) ideas to adorn and enhance your living spaces as a family, activities to keep the kids occupied and creative, and many simple home-style recipes to feed your favorite people. You'll read the tales behind creating each décor piece, inventing each parental survival tip, and cooking up each tasty dish. I've learned some invaluable strategies and a whole heck of a bunch of what-not-to-dos along the way, and I'm sharing all of that with you here.

One of the things I've learned over the years and want to make sure I pass along

Nothing grates my cheese more than spending money on DIY and crafting materials that I'm only going to use once!

to you is that "homemade" doesn't have to mean "completely original and difficult to make." I prefer to do things more along the "homemade(ish)" route of crafting and cooking. A combination of ready-made items and a-la-carte supplies can produce an end result that is uniquely crafted without breaking the bank or giving you a headache. And that's the guiding principle for every project, recipe, and tip in this book.

As we parents watch our children grow, we strive to be active participants in their lives, to raise them into good and happy young people. My hope is to inspire you with ways to spend valuable time with your children, teach them creativity and ingenuity, and whip up some deliciously caloric meals and painfully cute crafts along the way. Wherever you are on this crazy journey of parenthood, come with me as we go through a year of projects together that will bring joy and smiles to all the people in your house... including you!

Happy making!
Kristin

Kristin

Our Story

Kristin, Edward, Caroline, Nicoli, Austin, Matteo, Santo, Rosaline, Magdeline Mae, and Sebastian

When I married Edward, my life changed for the absolute best. We agreed to jump into this marriage thing head-on and take on life together for better for worse, for richer or for poorer. I am pretty sure we thought we would have a few kids and be so much "cooler" than our parents. But, like many young newlyweds, were we very wrong!

Here we are, more than a dozen years and eight kids later, raising our family a whole lot like our parents raised us. Our love, laughs, struggles, and failures have led us to healthy kids, a home we love, and a business that has taken me from a blog on your computer screen to appearing on your TV screen. (Hey, maybe I am cool!) The journey that got us here is one full of faith, creativity, and the motto "We are not quitters!"

OUR HOME

As our children grow, I watch our home evolve right along with them. It is ever-changing. When we bought the house more than a decade ago, it most definitely was not what

You figure out what makes you joyful, and make sure you do that as often as possible with as much zeal you can manage!

I would have considered my dream home. Sure, it had a lot going for it: the backyard was great, and it was in a quiet neighborhood in an amazing town. But it was a simple contractor-grade home from the '80s, and every room within its four walls lacked any sort of originality or detail. So, I decided to assign myself a mission: either make this stinkin' ugly house the home I envisioned it to be, or stop complaining about it.

From the outside, a home is just a house, brick and mortar, a structure. But it's the inside that counts—the interior is what truly makes the *home*. The feel and vibe of each room are a representation of the family unit living there. Regardless of what's trending in home décor or what this year's paint color is, I believe a cheerful home is one that encompasses the soul and vibrancy of every inhabitant—no matter if it's a house, an apartment, or a condo. With that in mind, I set out to make that the age-old saying "home is where the heart is" true of our house.

Easier said than done! For one, we didn't exactly have a home-improvement budget. We were pregnant with our #5, and I was staying at home with the kids. Also, I had zero experience in any aspect of renovation, and my knowledge of power tools was pretty much nada.

So, I started small. I knew I could work with a quart of paint or stain. I began collecting discarded furniture from family and friends and reimagining the items into what I wanted. I taught myself how to work a cordless drill and how to maneuver an orbital sander. When I felt comfortable in my new skin as a kick-butt maker of crap from junk is when I really started to experiment in my crafting and décor. It's also the moment I realized how very much my kids wanted to be hands-on involved in our home-improvement

My blog was born to serve as a means to record our crazy-train life and share our slightly imperfect home that's always chaotic but never not perfectly entertaining.

ventures too. And why the heck shouldn't they be? They live here as well!

BIRTH OF A BUSINESS

Starting a blog seemed like the ideal way to combine my passion for writing with my commitment to raising good humans and my proclivity for creativity. Hence, my blog was born—serving as a means to record our crazy-train life and share our slightly imperfect home that's always chaotic but never not perfectly entertaining.

To be honest, I didn't have a lot of confidence in the whole blog thing when I first began writing. I mean, who the heck would want to read about the crazy things going on in *my* life? I had absolutely no experience in writing, and I was doing things in my home that no one else was really doing in the décor world. But a very encouraging and persistent friend urged me to start the blog, and I eventually gave it a go. I created the blog under the radar—I didn't advertise it, I didn't share it, heck, I don't even think I told the kids about it at first! I considered it a virtual photo-filled journal (since I failed at the whole "scrapbook for each child" thing shortly after #3 was born). But what I absolutely never expected to happen was for it to become a blog read in multiple countries that would lead to a career that included television

Having an oversized family requires a colossal amount of patience, a massive sum of humility, and the distinct capability of being the loudest in a room full of yelling people.

and radio appearances, newspaper column writing, and authoring my very own book! It's both a humbling and incredible feeling when a fellow tired mama sends me a quick note to let me know one of my parental survival tips saved her day, or one of my DIY projects was everything she didn't know she needed in her home. One of my favorite quotes (by Deepak Chopra), "When you make a choice, you change the future," could not possibly be more apt!

FAMILY LOGISTICS

At this point, you might be wondering how I juggle all this—renovating, blogging, and keeping a family of eight kids and two parents afloat. In fact, I'm often asked, "How in the world do you manage to feed your family home-cooked meals every day?"

Having an oversized family is most definitely not for the faint of heart. It requires a colossal amount of patience, a massive sum of humility, and the distinct capability of being the loudest in a room full of yelling people. The knowledge that you must eat fast during dinner if you want a second serving is also very helpful.

Not many people choose to have large broods these days. Just a trip to the store as a fam of ten is proof of that. Exiting the Gam-bus (what we call our fifteen-passenger family van), parading in the doors, grabbing multiple shopping carts, corralling the younger kids, and wrangling the older ones makes it feel like the circus has come to town. The term "divide and conquer" is typically our MO when shopping with the whole gang. Basically, it's "Operation: Get What We Need and Get the Heck Out." Head counting is continual and bathroom stops are inevitable. It's an exhausting and overwhelming experience for everyone involved. I can only imagine how passersby feel!

I'm sure it's no surprise that feeding so many mouths takes a lot out of our budget, second only to our mortgage. Eating meals at home, purchasing in bulk, choosing off-brand products, and growing as much of our own produce as possible is key to keeping my family fed. Also of paramount importance is menu planning and a snack schedule—otherwise, the kids would eat All. Day. Long! Good ol' Shakespeare probably had no idea how right he was when he penned the phrase, "He hath eaten me out of house and home." No words could better describe what these kids would do if they were given free range in the kitchen all day every day!

WRAPPING IT UP

And there you have it. The things we've crafted to make our home our own, blog ramblings and experiences, and feeding my crew led to the projects, ideas, and recipes in this book.

Before I let you loose on these pages, I want you to keep this in mind... Someone once told me that "puffy paint is extinct in the craft world." I about choked to death on my sixth cup of lukewarm coffee! I had never heard anything so ludicrous in my life. Puffy paint is the glitter to my glam, the yin to my yang, the light to my day! OK, maybe I'm being a tad bit dramatic. The point is, what one person deems as outdated or unnecessary, another may view as timeless and essential. You figure out what makes

you joyful, and make sure you do that as often as possible with as much zeal you can manage. As for me, I'm sticking to my favorite oversized '90s puffy-paint iron-on Halloween sweatshirt until the seams literally cannot hold the outrageously decorated fabric together any longer!

In all seriousness, one thing is certain. When our children are ready to fly the coop, Edward and I will be able to let them loose knowing that they have acquired the basic survival skills. We pray our children will leave this home we've created for them as well-loved, well-rounded individuals that are capable of sharing their time, talent, and space with those around them. Along with a healthy dose of conflict resolution and the competence to create a healthy(ish) meal using minimal ingredients, I will rest easy knowing they are able to care for themselves and make good choices (at least most of the time)!

Eating meals at home, purchasing in bulk, choosing off-brand products, and growing as much of our own produce as possible is key to keeping my family fed.

CHAPTER 1

Spring Break

Ahh, springtime. We all know the age-old adages pertaining to the spring season—the beauty of change and new beginnings and all that flowery jazz full of fuzzy baby chicks and adorable tiny bunnies. The air is lighter, everyone's steps are peppier, and the world seems brighter (even if we're still walking around in dirty, snowy slush here in the Midwest for what seems like forever). It's a time for spring cleaning, colorful projects, and getting outside. In this section of the book, you'll find the projects, recipes, and ideas I've learned along the way to make the most of the season.

My family typically stays home during the week of spring break itself. Instead of a vacation, we take advantage of some overdue cleaning around the house as well as the garage and shed. It's definitely not the most enjoyable activity to partake in. Once we've finished the hard work, though, we have F-U-N. Our best-loved annual springtime activity is one that Edward and I made up years ago. We call it "Park Palooza," and here's how it goes.

After we've completed all the cleaning, we make a checklist of every local playground in the area. We pack up snacks and drinks, load the kids in the Gam-bus (our fifteen-passenger family van), and head to the first park on the tally. Setting a timer, we typically give the kids thirty minutes or so to run around, slide to their hearts' content, and swing like animals on the monkey bars. When the time's up, we pile back into the van and move on to the next park on the list, continuing until the kiddos are sweaty, worn out, and too tired to play anymore. When it comes down to it, any situation—even spring cleaning—can be enjoyable with the right mindset and a little creativity. You can make great memories without spending a dime by simply giving the kids your time and attention.

Embellished Umbrella

SUPPLIES

- Plain white umbrella
- 5 yards (4.5m) mini pom-pom ball fringe trim
- Hot glue
- Fabric puffy paint
- Round sponge brushes (various sizes)
- Paint palette or plate

TIP

You can use acrylic paint in place of fabric puffy paint. Acrylic paint is water-soluble when wet, but it becomes water-resistant when dry.

I have come to understand that nothing ensures my kids will sleep well at night quite like a day of playing outside. I live for the nights when their little cherub heads hit the pillow and they instantly fall into a sweet dreamland. Unfortunately, these peaceful and uneventful evenings are few and far between at my house. For some reason unbeknownst to me, Mr. Sandman has left my husband and me high and dry to tame these wild and tireless animals on our own.

Difficult bedtimes are why we try to encourage the kids to play outside even in the winter snow or the summer showers. They need to get outside and move around, to run and bike and skate and jump, to expel even the slightest bit of that cooped-up energy. And playing outside, stomping around in muddy puddles, means that the crafty-crazy in me wants to give them a cute umbrella to keep them dry, naturally! This embellished umbrella is the perfect way for your kiddos to add their own style to an otherwise plain wet-weather accessory.

Make playing in spring showers more fun with an umbrella customized with your kiddo's favorite colors.

1 **Paint the initial dots.** Prepare a palette (or plate) with large pools of puffy paint in different colors. With the umbrella open, paint polka dots across the top of the fabric. (I used different-sized sponge brushes for different colors.)

2 **Use good dot-making technique.** When using the round sponge brushes, keep the handle straight up and down while you twist it into the paint you wish to use. You want the sponge to be saturated but not heavily covered. Approaching the umbrella surface at a 90-degree angle, apply the sponge while pushing the round tip flat.

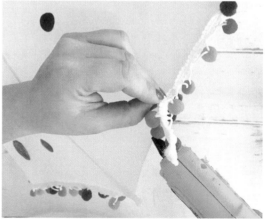

3 **Fill in the dots.** Once you've made your polka dots, fill them in with more puffy paint straight from the bottle to add the dimension and thickness that puffy paint typically provides. Making the shapes with the sponges first ensures that your circles will be the desired sizes and perfectly round.

4 **Add trim.** Allow the paint to fully dry (for about two or three hours). Then hot glue pom-pom trim along the bottom edge of the umbrella, working just a few inches (several centimeters) at a time.

Mommy Daddy Nights

I get a lot of questions regarding how we manage our time with our tribe. One of the most important things Edward and I started doing almost a decade ago that has helped all of us with this conundrum is Mommy Daddy Nights. Each child gets a night to have Edward and I all to him- or herself while everyone else goes to bed. That's fifteen to twenty minutes of extra time, one-on-one talking, reading, telling jokes, playing "I Spy," etc.—whatever the child wants to do. The kids truly look forward to their time sans siblings with our undivided attention!

WHY I DON'T GIVE SLEEP ADVICE

Typically, our bedtime routine consists of something akin to this:

- a minimum of four tuck-ins (because they've realized they had to use the bathroom four separate times in an hour—and this is after we've made them go right before the first tuck-in);
- two bedtime stories;
- four sips of water (taken after each bathroom trip, of course);
- and finally, that really important "something I have to ask you right now, Mom," which winds up being an inquiry regarding either (a) the number of days until their next birthday; (b) the days, hours, minutes, and seconds until their next birthday; or (c) why Santa Claus wears red.
- Oh, and we certainly cannot forget the every-single-night "Can I please, puhleeeeze sleep with you and Daddy?" question.

Tater Tot Casserole

INGREDIENTS

- 2–3 lbs. ground beef
- 1 tsp. garlic salt
- Three 10-oz. cans condensed cream of mushroom soup
- 1 cup half-and-half or milk
- ½ cup salted butter, melted
- 2 tbsp. grated Parmesan cheese
- 4 cups shredded cheddar cheese, divided
- 32 oz. frozen Tater Tots (also known as potato puffs)

This Tater Tot casserole is old-school cuisine with a cafeteria flare that will never go out of style. Just like denim and Wayfarer sunglasses, it's here forever. My Aunt Trish would make it often when all the cousins were together at her house, running amok and getting into trouble (back in the '80s, when staying outside unless you had to pee or eat was a rule, and finding mischief was a given). The fact that that woman had all of us kids over to her house all the time is a mystery to my adult mind. She was and still is a saint who, to this day, adores children and has the patience and love of Mother Teresa.

Whether you find yourself hosting your own gaggle of hungry kids, or you're lucky enough to be feeding a tamer crowd that's a bit less hangry, this simple and cheesy dish is easy to double or triple on a dime. For nostalgic purposes, try serving it on a cafeteria tray!

Give a freezer bag of potato puffs new life with a few inexpensive pantry staples.

INSTRUCTIONS

1. Grease a 9" x 13" (23 x 33cm) baking dish and preheat oven to 350°F (175°C).
2. Brown beef in garlic salt.
3. Mix soup, cooked beef, half-and-half (or milk), melted butter, Parmesan cheese, and 2 cups of shredded cheddar in large bowl.
4. Pour mixture into baking dish.
5. Layer Tater Tots evenly over mixture.
6. Top with remaining 2 cups shredded cheddar.
7. Sprinkle a little more Parmesan on top (because why the heck not!).
8. Cover with tinfoil and bake for 45 minutes or until Tater Tots are hot.

Pet Silhouette

SUPPLIES

- Side/profile view photo of pet
- Colorful cardstock
- Pencil
- Sharp scissors or hobby/craft knife
- 8" x 12" (20 x 30.5cm) wood plaque
- White spray paint or acrylic craft paint
- Black marker
- White pen
- Clear-drying glue stick
- Decoupage medium
- Foam paintbrush

One of my favorite DIY projects will always and forevermore be the monochromatic silhouette portraits I created of my kids. I utterly adore the pouty lips, rounded chins, and genetically passed-down upturned tips of noses I see in the shadowed outlines. (About those sniffers: sorry, kiddos. That's totally my genes. No matter how many times you smoosh that schnozzle down, it will unceasingly be pointed up.) Essentially, their wonderfully and uniquely made facial characteristics are freeze-framed in that moment of time. There's no distraction from background images or those stinkin' skinny jeans with huge holes (totally not earned from years of hard work) that my teenagers insist on wearing. Just the curves and angles of those much-loved angelic kissers.

But I eventually realized that our family wall really wasn't complete without our two loony pooches. After all, these hairy boys provide our home with lively comic relief and an endless supply of wet kisses. They work hard to make sure we all know how much we're loved around here on the daily. These stinky dogs certainly take their job of friendship, loyalty, and guarding us from the big bad mailman very seriously every day. The whole neighborhood is fully aware that our house is fiercely protected by two pint-sized watchdogs that will attack with fearsome tongue licks from the ankles down whenever necessary. Man's best friend, indeed.

As a sort of official recognition of their important role in our lives, I crafted these colorful pet silhouettes. As a bonus, you can use the same method for making silhouettes of human family members too!

LOVE
BEGINS
AT
HOME

This project works perfectly for kid silhouettes as well, so feel free to turn the whole family into art!

INSTRUCTIONS

1 **Take the picture.** Get a good, clear profile view of your pet. Make sure he is in front of an unadorned, light-colored wall and facing sideways. If you are having a hard time getting your rascally dog to stay still, a spoonful of peanut butter will get his attention (and give you a funny tongue for the picture too!).

2 **Print out the picture.** Adjust the photo to a 5" x 7" (12.5 x 17.5cm) size in your printer settings. Print out the photo on computer paper using the black and white option.

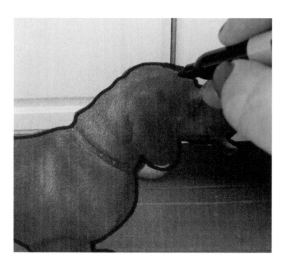

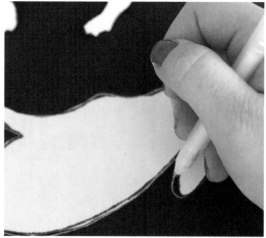

3 **Cut out the silhouette.** Trace your pet's outline with a black marker, then cut out around the outline with scissors or a hobby/craft knife.

4 **Trace the cutout.** Trace around the cutout image onto the black cardstock using a white pen.

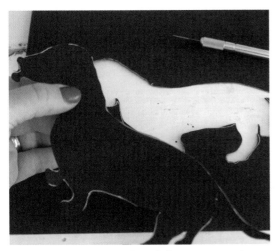

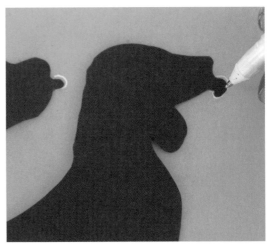

5 **Cut the tracing.** Carefully cut around the outline of the pet until you have a complete cardstock cutout.

6 **Paint the plaque.** Paint the entire wood plaque using white spray paint (in a well-ventilated area) or acrylic craft paint and a foam paintbrush. Allow it to fully dry. While it's drying, trace the tongue outline onto pink or red cardstock and cut it out.

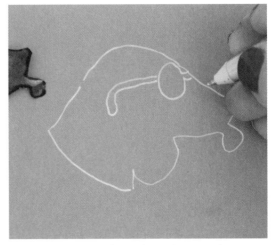

7 **Assemble the portrait.** Using a glue stick, glue the pet profile cutout onto the white plaque. Glue the little tongue in place as well.

8 **Add personal touches.** Jazz up the plaque by cutting out colorful bow ties, bandanas, collars, bugs, grass, or sun from bright cardstock and adding them to your pet's silhouette using the glue stick.

9 **Draw on final details.** Use a permanent marker to add final touches like the bee's flight trail shown here.

10 **Cover with a layer of decoupage medium.** With a foam paintbrush, add a coat of decoupage medium over the top of the entire plaque for protection. Allow it to fully dry.

TIP

It's a breeze to make raindrops with a hole punch!

Eggshell Planting

First line up clean, empty eggshell halves in a thin cardboard box.

Fill with soil, add seeds, stick in some Popsicle stick plant labels so you remember what's what, and get ready to plant in the garden come summer!

Did you know that eggshells make great starter containers for your summer vegetable seeds? Eggshells are made up almost entirely of calcium carbonate, which just happens to be one of the most essential nutrients for thriving plants! You simply plant your vegetable seeds in the shells in the spring and transplant the vessel (egg and started plant) into the garden at the beginning of summer. As the shells break down, they enrich the soil with the calcium and nitrogen. The plants' roots absorb them and use them to grow strong.

As a family living in the suburbs, we actually keep some pet chickens, enjoying their fresh eggs in our meals. It has taught my family how to be good stewards of the planet—from feeding the chickens our leftover meal scraps that would otherwise be tossed out, to reusing the droppings to provide nutrients to our garden soil. If you want to keep chickens, you'll need poop boots. For an easy storage solution for our yucky boots, we hang them upside down on old wood spindles that we drove into the ground. The rain keeps the undersides of the boots somewhat clean, and the spindles keep the pairs together.

Hang boots upside down on old wood spindles!

Dog Treats

INGREDIENTS

- 1½ cups uncooked oatmeal
- 1 large banana
- ½ cup xylitol-free creamy peanut butter (xylitol is toxic to dogs)

Even the slobbery, hairy four-legged kids in our lives deserve a special snack occasionally. Sure, you can go to the pet-supply store and buy something premade from the plastic bins by the checkout lanes, but it's crazy easy to whip something up at home for them too. And you'll get more bang for your buck by baking these babies up yourself. Plus, only three ingredients and easy prep work means the human kids can be completely hands-on while making this treat for their best canine friends!

INSTRUCTIONS

1. Preheat oven to 350°F (175°C).
2. Using a food processor, grind oatmeal to a powder. Set aside a tablespoon or so of ground oats.
3. In a large bowl, mix ground oats, banana, and peanut butter until combined.
4. Roll dough to ¼" (0.5cm) thickness on a surface dusted with the extra ground oats. If the dough seems too dry to roll, add a bit more peanut butter to the mixture.
5. Cut dough into small pieces or use a cookie cutter to make shapes.
6. Bake in preheated oven for 15 minutes or until edges begin to brown.

Even if you don't have a dog, you probably know someone who does! Make these for your friends' furry friends.

A rainy afternoon with a bunch of bored kids is a great time to make some treats for the dog.

Tin Can Art Storage

SUPPLIES

- Tin cans (with labels removed)
- Decorative napkins
- Decoupage medium
- Foam paintbrush
- Mini pom-pom ball fringe trim
- Hot glue gun
- Scissors

Color coordinate markers and colored pencils in a super-simple project that repurposes tin cans and napkins.

I'm a wee bit obsessed with new ways to organize all our junk (because we have a ton of junk). I also believe it's important to involve the kids when we are cleaning up a common space in the house. After all, it's typically their stuff I'm trying to sort and arrange, which unfortunately means they also typically have some strange personal attachment to the items I'm cleaning out. Like that random broken crayon that was lost for who knows how long under the desk that also just happens to be their "favorite crayon in the world." And we cannot forget the dust bunny–covered dried marker without a cap that they "love, Love, LOVE to color with." After these confessions of undying affection for items that belong at the bottom of the trash can, I find, is a good moment to discuss the importance of taking care of your things; the importance of having a place for everything and everything having a place; the importance of being able to find what you need when you need it. Solid advice, right?

Of course, as per tradition, at this point in the family-time endeavor, I've been gifted with an obscene amount of dramatic eye rolls and a few heavy puffs of irritated teen air. The older ones may even throw out a few reminders of their own. Like, "Remember that time Mom couldn't find her glasses because they were on her head?" or "Remember when Mom was looking everywhere for her phone and she couldn't find it because she was talking on it?" All of these result in quite a few giggles and chuckles because "Mom loses her stuff all the time too." Hardy-har-har, kids.

It was actually during one such day in particular, when I was searching for marker tops and sharpening broken colored pencils, that I thought of this organizing idea. I don't know about you, but I love a good repurposed project. Heck, I was repurposing junk before repurposing junk was considered cool—and these cans full of color-coordinated art supplies are the definition of cool. They look cute sitting all together on the dining room table and make it so easy for the little ones to figure out which color goes where!

This is a good project to discuss the importance of taking care of your things; the importance of having a place for everything and everything having a place; the importance of being able to find what you need when you need it.

INSTRUCTIONS

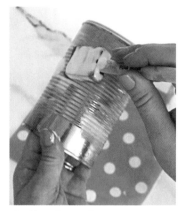

1 **Brush on decoupage medium.** On the outside surface of a clean, dry tin can, brush on a layer of decoupage medium using a foam paintbrush.

2 **Wrap the napkin.** Carefully wrap the napkin, design side facing out, around the outside of the can, making sure the edge of the napkin is flush with the bottom of the can. If necessary, add more decoupage on the can to help the napkin stick.

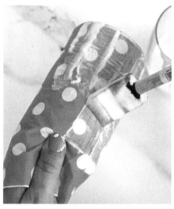

3 **Add more decoupage medium.** Paint a new, thick layer of decoupage medium all over the outside of the napkin-wrapped can.

TIP

I use 2-ply napkins for my cans. It gives a thicker coverage and allows for a slouchy end look that I find cute. If you peel apart and separate the plies before attaching them, use only the decorated layers. Separate single plies of napkin will hug the can for a tighter appearance, but they will also show any ridges in the can and appear less opaque.

4 **Trim excess napkin.** Trim the overhanging napkin from the can, cutting neatly along the top rim.

5 **Add the fringe.** Hot glue a length of pom-pom fringe trim around the top rim.

Art Display

Old picture frames make an awesome display for artwork in the kitchen! If the doors of your fridge are full to the max with colorful crayon illustrations, and you've got nowhere else to pin up your junior Picasso's priceless pieces, this is the solution for you. Pop out the glass from a frame, replace it with a piece of corkboard hot glued to the interior, and use removable wall hanging strips to adhere the back of the frame to your cabinet door.

When you run out of room on the fridge, make the most of other flat surfaces with quick-change corkboard displays.

No-Bake Energy Balls

INGREDIENTS

- 3 cups old-fashioned quick oats
- ¼ cup coconut flakes
- ¼ cup chocolate chips
- 1 cup peanut butter
- 1 cup hazelnut cocoa spread
- ½ cup honey

These balls of sweet goodness are an essential part of our school year. I love them because they are fast to throw together for an afternoon snack or special treat without having to turn on the oven, and the kiddos love them because they are so gosh darn pop-in-your-mouth good! These treats will provide your small athlete that extra boost of energy that comes in handy right before a big game or a hard practice and are the perfect size for on-the-go snacking. You can make them bite-sized or larger, and they're not as sticky as you might think.

Truly, anything goes with this recipe. Add flaxseed, wheat germ, cinnamon, peanut butter chips, butterscotch chips—or omit ingredients I have listed if someone has an allergy or simply doesn't like something.

TIP

I have mixed the ingredients for these treats by hand with a spoon, with a hand mixer, and by using my stand mixer if I'm tripling the recipe and feeding a crowd. Any mixing method will work; the key is for the batter to be thick and sticky at the end—sticky enough to form balls with your hands.

INSTRUCTIONS

1. Mix dry ingredients (oats, coconut flakes, and chocolate chips).
2. Add wet ingredients (peanut butter, hazelnut cocoa spread, and honey).
3. Stir until dry ingredients are completely and evenly coated.
4. Form into ball shapes and place on wax paper or serving tray.

Rainbow Centerpiece

SUPPLIES

- Rainbow pack of satin headbands
- Styrofoam craft balls in various sizes: 2" (5cm), 1" (2.5cm), and ¾" (2cm)
- Miniature rubber bands
- Two 1" (2.5cm) metal corner braces
- 6" x 12" (15 x 30.5cm) pine wood base
- Hot glue gun
- Phillips screwdriver (optional)
- Two ½" (1.5cm) wood screws (optional)
- Acrylic paint (optional)
- Paintbrush (optional)

Around these parts, we go gaga over rainbows! Walking outside after a good spring soaking and discovering that tapestry of splendor in the sky never ceases to amaze us. And for as much as this big girl would love to actually find the big pot of gold treasure at the end of those beautiful rings (hello, paid-off bills, I'll see you in my dreams), I have to admit that experiencing the excitement pouring out of my kiddos every time they spy a pretty rainbow among the clouds is most definitely worth its weight in gold. And honestly, if those moments of awe and amazement in their little eyes are not a treasure to behold, I sure as heck don't know what is. I guess that explains why rainbows are associated with happiness and hope, right? The colors join in an arch of proof that miracles can happen, even after a storm. Those primary colors all lined up just the right way screams pure joy to my '80s-child, rainbow-leg-warmer-lovin' soul.

And what could be better than enjoying all the bright and showy colors of the rainbow outside? Enjoying the bright and showy colors of the rainbow *inside* on your family table, o' course! This rainbow centerpiece will bring all sorts of happy-go-lucky feelings into your home. Oh, and believe you me, the fact that the entirety of this ROY-G-BIV awesomeness can be created in less than ten minutes, using hair supplies you probably already have lying around (or can quickly pick up at the drugstore around the corner), is nothing more than magical crafting at work, friends.

We love spotting rainbows after rain showers! Bring that joy to the dining room table with this quick craft.

This makes a great gift to bring some cheer to the table when someone invites your family over!

INSTRUCTIONS

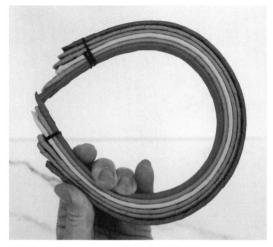

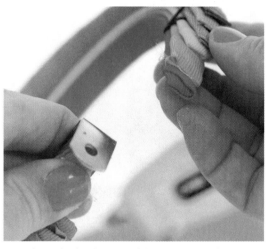

1 **Arrange the headbands.** Place your headbands in ROY-G-BIV order. Then attach them at the ends in a stack as shown using miniature rubber bands. I find it easier to attach a few at a time, using multiple mini rubber bands, until they are all lined up.

2 **Attach the braces.** Using more rubber bands, secure the headbands to a corner brace on each side. Then hot glue each corner brace to the interior bottom of the stack of headbands for additional stability.

3 **Glue to braces to the base.** Hot glue each brace bottom to the wood base. Alternatively, screw the braces into the base. (Note: If you want to paint the base, do so and allow it to dry before attaching the braces.)

4 **Add the large balls.** Hot glue all of the largest Styrofoam balls around the base of the headbands, forming a roughly triangular shape.

5 **Add the small balls.** Randomly glue the smaller Styrofoam balls in and around the large balls to finish the illusion of exaggerated, puffy clouds.

Drinking Glass Flower Vase

No matter what the season, my kids love to bring me their found treasures from the yard or their walks around the neighborhood with Daddy. Sometimes it's a crisp, freshly fallen leaf; other times it's a newly bloomed tulip; and most of the time it's a handful of pretty weed blossoms. Of course, after the big presentation, those little eyes will continue to stare at me with anticipation until the precious offerings are safely in water and placed on the windowsill for all to see. It just so happens that a simple drinking glass is the perfect size to hold these bitty bouquets! If you have a selection of underused glasses to choose from, you could even let your child pick the perfect match for their offering.

Carrot Cake

INGREDIENTS

- 2 cups white sugar
- 1 cup vegetable oil
- 4 large eggs
- Two 4½-oz. jars carrot baby food
- 1 tsp. vanilla extract
- 2 cups all-purpose flour
- ½ tsp. salt
- 1½ tsp. baking soda
- ¼ tsp. ground cloves
- ¼ tsp. ground nutmeg
- 2 tsp. ground cinnamon

For the frosting:
- 8 oz. cream cheese, softened
- ½ cup salted butter, softened
- 1 tbsp. vanilla extract
- 4 cups confectioners' sugar, sifted
- 1¼ cups chopped pecans (optional)

We've all heard of or experienced our share of dinnertime horror stories—the accounts of unfortunate parents whose kiddos flat-out refuse to eat anything served, or the mom who makes multiple meals a night to appease her picky brood. FYI: I'm a "you're going to eat what I make" mom. As in, you either eat it or you go to bed hungry, because after this meal is cleaned up, the Kitchen. Is. Closed. (Sort of; I mean, I may let them have a piece of cheese or a few slices of apple before bed if they ate absolutely nothing—I'm not *that* mean.)

I'm relieved to say that my kids aren't necessarily persnickety about meals per se—well, except for the one child of my loins who literally created his first haiku poem at three years old to lament his utter disappointment in my dinners. And I quote: "Corn and beans. Corn and beans. Every day it's corn and beans." The corn was pronounced "torn," and the ditty was performed with a pronounced lip pout accompanied by footed pajama stomps. The verse was actually quite catchy in a daycare open-mic poetry slam kind of way. And unbeknownst to the downcast small fry at the time, those three short sentences of his have forever been added to our bucket of funny family stories. You know what I'm talking about—the tales that are brought up and laughed about over and over again at the family table through the years. The yarn that becomes the very threads that hold the whole gosh darn family history together.

The good news is, he's been the only one of eight kids who has ever really given me a hard time about eating veggies. The bad news is that, almost ten years later, he still feels exactly the same. Collectively, though, there seems to be only one general food aversion that my entire brood agrees on: if you throw chunks in a food they consider to be "smooth" or "creamy," they are *not* on board for taste testing. Tomatoes in the spaghetti sauce? Big nope. Peanuts in the peanut butter? Heck to the no. Carrot pieces in a carrot cake? Nix that idea before you even start baking. That's why my fam-favorite carrot cake is made using baby food instead of grated carrots. You read that right! A few jars of baby food, and the result is moist and most definitely *not* gag-worthy chunky in the slightest.

INSTRUCTIONS

1. Preheat oven to 350°F (175°C).
2. Grease and flour two 9" (23cm) round cake pans.
3. Using a stand mixer or a large bowl and hand mixer, combine sugar and oil. Add eggs, carrot baby food, and 1 tsp. vanilla. Beat until mixture is smooth.
4. In a separate bowl, combine flour, salt, baking soda, and spices.
5. Slowly add the dry mix to the creamed mix and beat well.
6. Pour batter into two prepared pans.
7. Bake for 30–35 minutes or until a toothpick inserted in the center of the cake comes out clean.

To prepare the frosting:

1. Beat cream cheese and butter in a mixer on high until light and fluffy.
2. Add 1 tbsp. vanilla and the sifted confectioners' sugar. Start beating on low, slowly increasing the speed of the mixer until the frosting is smooth and chunk-free.
3. If using pecans, you can fold them into the frosting at this time or use them as a garnish on the top of the fully frosted cake.

I totally "baby" my picky eaters with a secret ingredient in this family favorite.

Sidewalk Popsicle Chalk

SUPPLIES

- Plaster powder (purchase from a local craft store or make your own—see Tip on page 43)
- Hot water
- Food coloring
- Silicone Popsicle molds (hard plastic Popsicle molds can work too, but it is a bit more difficult for the chalk to release from the walls)
- Nonstick cooking spray

Yes, you really can make sidewalk chalk at home!

One of our most favorite sunny day activities is to chalk up every square inch of concrete, brick, and patio available outside with doodles, block letters, drawings, and stick figures. Therefore, my family goes through copious amounts of sidewalk chalk. And the only thing better than creating something with colorful sidewalk chalk is creating something with colorful sidewalk chalk that you made yourself!

This sidewalk chalk recipe came about in the midst of the COVID-19 pandemic. It was spring, the weather had warmed, the last of the snow piles had melted, and I could finally let the little monsters loose outside to run free and ride bikes without dressing them in layers as thick as the Stay Puft Marshmallow Man. And let me tell you, when my kids play outside, they *play outside*. This daily activity from March through November involves removing every single hula hoop, ball, scooter, odd rope piece, and random shoe out of our garage and making sure they're efficiently spread across the entire expanse of our front lawn, giving the impression we've been hit by some sort of a toy cyclone. (I'm confident that since we've moved into our home, we've brought our neighborhood's house values down. Oops. And *this* is why we deliver Christmas cookies every year while singing horribly out-of-tune Christmas carols to all the surrounding homes on our street. So far, no one has called the cops on us for hoarding or for violation of city ordinances, so our tactic must be working!)

Anyway, on this particular spring day, we had played our way through all the toys and had effectively gone through our entire chalk supply. We needed a quick DIY solution for a sidewalk chalk refill. Using our Popsicle molds from the pantry, we made our very own uniquely colored, custom sidewalk Popsicle chalk. Bonus: each chalk-sicle lasted well over a week!

When you've played with every possible toy and need something new to entertain, make this colorful set of homemade chalks.

INSTRUCTIONS

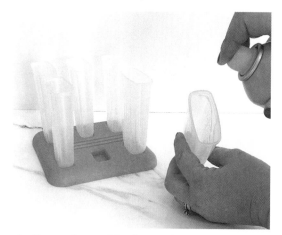

1 **Spray the molds.** Spray the inside of each Popsicle mold liberally with nonstick cooking spray.

2 **Measure the ingredients.** Measure 2 cups of plaster powder and 1 cup of hot water. Do this separately for each different color you want to make.

TIPS

✓ Make sure you clean up safely! Dispose of the mixing supplies, or clean the containers and utensils outside with a garden hose or bucket of soapy water. Do not rinse or flush any of the plaster mix down your household drains—it could harden and create a blockage.

✓ For an easier release, run each Popsicle mold under hot water for one minute to allow more flexibility in the mold. This will help the chalk shape loosen and pop out.

✓ You can make your own homemade plaster powder if you can't purchase it. It doesn't make quite as hardy chalk, but it still works! To make your own plaster powder, add 1 cup of hot water to 2 cups of white flour, mixing with a spoon or spatula. Continue stirring until there are no lumps and the plaster is thick but not difficult to stir.

3 **Mix the ingredients.** Mix the plaster powder and water together in a disposable container, using a plastic spoon or wooden Popsicle stick, until you have a smooth, soupy consistency.

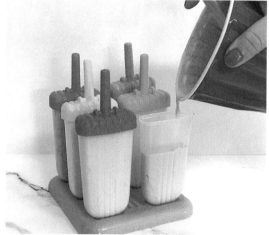

4 **Add color.** Add seven to ten drops of food coloring and mix thoroughly.

5 **Pour mix into molds.** Pour the colored mixture into the molds. Here's a fun twist: try filling each mold with layers of different-colored plaster instead of one single color. Allow 24 hours to dry.

Popsicle Stick Numbers

"It's my turn!" "I want to go first!" "Why can't I ever be first?" "Who gets to go first?" "Can I go next?"

Every parent has felt the familiar sharp edge of insanity that these questions produce in the temporal lobe. I mean, it's hard enough just making sure your children stay alive every day. Who has time to remember who was the last one to brush his or her teeth first in the downstairs bathroom (morning and evening, because, you know, it's different)? Or who sat in the third chair from the left in the second row of the van last?

I discovered a solution to the "take turns" chaos that ensues in my home every day, all day, at all times. I needed a break from trying to remember who exactly went first last time, or the time before that, or the time before that time. This little jar of sticks trick wound up being my savior, my breath of "fair" air. And all you need to make your own is Popsicle sticks. Number a Popsicle stick for each little one that "never gets to go first," throw them in a jar of any sort, and voilà! Everyone takes a turn pulling a stick, and your number is YOUR NUMBER in line! You can't argue with random chance. Throw the jar in your purse, take in the car for those extra-long rides, or keep it in the kitchen for easy access.

Chocolate Chip Oatmeal Banana Bars

INGREDIENTS

- 2 cups sugar
- ⅔ cup salted butter, softened
- 4 large eggs
- 3 cups (6 medium) ripe bananas, mashed
- ⅔ cup water
- 3⅓ cups flour
- 2 tsp. baking soda
- 1 tsp. salt
- ½ tsp. baking powder
- 1 cup milk chocolate chips
- ½ cup chopped walnuts (optional)

For the oat topping:
- 2 cups old-fashioned quick oats
- 4 tbsp. salted butter
- 2 tbsp. brown sugar
- 2 tsp. vanilla
- 1 tsp. cinnamon

Baking is a sort of love language I share with my family. In a way, it's how I let them know that I've been thinking of all my people all day. And I must confess, the excitement I hear when they first walk through the door in the afternoon and get a whiff of whatever I've got in the oven makes me totally confident in my ability to "bake" them happy. I'm a firm believer that there's nothing a homemade baked goodie and a big, warm hug can't fix. First-day-of-school jitters? Cookies will handle that. Upcoming school test anxiety? Yep, better start mixing that batter. Monday blues? How about a little something sweet to help you get through the morning?

I whipped up these chocolate chip oatmeal banana bars on a Sunday night after dinner cleanup. Mondays are hard, and Sunday evenings can easily set the tone for the next day. The kids were crazy delighted to go to bed that evening, knowing that they were going to have a super special breakfast before school the next morning. A little bit of work on my part the day before meant a smidge-easier A.M. routine—and a whole bunch of smiling faces and full bellies on their way to the bus.

Baking is a sort of love language I share with my family.

INSTRUCTIONS

1. Heat oven to 350°F (175°C).
2. Grease the bottom of a 9" x 13" (23 x 33cm) baking pan.
3. In your mixer, blend sugar and butter until creamy.
4. Mix in eggs.
5. Add bananas and water.
6. Slowly add dry ingredients (flour, baking soda, salt, and baking powder) to prevent spillover.
7. Fold in chocolate chips (and walnuts if using).
8. Pour batter into prepared pan.
9. Prepare topping by browning oats in butter, brown sugar, vanilla, and cinnamon on stovetop over low heat.
10. Sprinkle oat topping over batter.
11. Bake 30–35 minutes or until a toothpick inserted in the center comes out clean.

GROUP ACTIVITIES & FEEDING A CROWD

FUN AND TASTY IDEAS FOR EVERY DAY

Lord knows everything I do for my family is supersized. The capacity of our washing machine (commercial-grade, because we'd burn the motor out of anything else), the serving portions of our meals, and the number of shoes on my garage floor on any given day are all proof positive that we are living life in bulk. I'm sure there's also a joke in here somewhere regarding the size of my pants, but we'll leave that one between me and my elastic waistband.

Even though our days look a little different than the average American home's, there are times when my recipes for feeding a crowd or tips for entertaining a gaggle of kids can come in handy for anyone, no matter how big or small their own family is. They allow many people to join in, they're easy to organize while wrangling everyone, and (if applicable) they produce sufficiently tasty calories for each hungry child and big person around.

Park Palooza
(page 12)

Tater Tot Casserole
(page 18)

Popsicle Stick Numbers
(page 45)

Lemonade Stand
(page 50)

S'mores Station
(page 81)

Fancy Crust, All-Butter Piecrust, and Perfectly Perfect Apple Pie
(pages 105–108)

ALL THINGS ORGANIZATIONAL

MAKING YOUR HOUSE A HOME AND CONTROLLING THE CLUTTER

Keeping my home neat and tidy is a constant battle of wills between me and my home's cohabitants. I try my darndest to ensure we start each day with cabinets, countertops, and rooms organized and functional while my kids try their hardest to crush any hopes and dreams I had of order and structure. The single socks stuffed into the couch cushions, the crumbs and sticky spots everywhere, and the inability of anyone to actually spit the toothpaste *into* the sink are just a few of my daily struggles that I'm sure any parent can relate to. So, if I come up with an idea to organize that's not only cute, but functional and maybe a little amusing too, I'm going to give it a go on the off chance that it *might* work. These projects and ideas are not only enjoyable to make, but they will elevate your home décor to the next level while serving to reduce (but not eliminate— never eliminate!) the clutter that comes with kids.

Jack-o'-Lantern Candy Holder
(page 94)

Game Day
(page 115)

Cup Tray
(page 127)

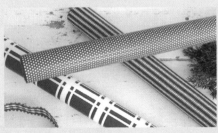

Gift Wrap Matters
(page 147)

Tin Can Art Storage
(page 28)

Art Display
(page 31)

Silver Storage
(page 153)

CHAPTER 2

Kicking Off a Creative Summer

Oh, sweet, sweet summer. The perpetual dog days of staying up late, sleeping in, and having no plans on the weekly chalkboard calendar other than swimming and eating a considerable amount of snacks every afternoon. The kids count down the days and hours leading up to the very minute they can hop off the school bus for the last time, burn their homework in a huge bonfire out back, and make a mad dash to stop the ice cream truck as it jingles its catchy tunes in front of the house. Packing the camper for our maiden voyage of the season begins, lemonade stand plans get rolling, and we reacquaint ourselves with the workers at the little seasonal ice cream stand down the road (as we're repeat, big-spending customers, it's important for them to recognize their elite clientele, after all).

To keep us on task, we devise a summer checklist created from a tall frame full of summer-themed scrapbook paper strips. We use a dry-erase marker to record a list of all the things we want to do during the sunny and warm weeks of total academic freedom. From bike riding and creek walking to balmy nights playing Ghost in the Graveyard and catching fireflies, the hours are full of everything and nothing, and it's totally summer-tastic.

Our summer checklist sets the tone for the whole season and gets checked off item by item!

A lemonade stand is a great way to get to know your neighbors!

25¢

Bubblegum Machine

SUPPLIES

- 4" (10cm) plastic snow globe
- Red plastic cup
- Black plastic spoon
- Gumballs
- Hot glue gun
- Scissors

Gumball machines aren't just for gum! If you'd rather not risk a sticky situation like gum in your child's hair, use this same technique for other small treats.

My kids are split down the middle when it comes to the subject of whether I am the best classroom Room Mom. This is a title that most of us underslept, overbearing mothers take very seriously. Like, "chocolate fountain with loads of freshly cut fruit, mounds of marshmallows, piles of pretzels, stacks of spongy angel food cake, and heaps of freshly baked cookies on the side" seriously. (Don't judge. The intent was to completely buy the teacher's love, prove I was way better than Mrs. L's Room Mom "Karen" in the class next door, and make all the other teachers *wish* my kid was in their class. And I'm pretty confident it worked. Friends in high places, you know?)

While a few of my kiddos think I've earned the title "The Coolest Room Mom Ever" (these are obviously my favorite kiddos), there are a few that think I'm more of "The Most Embarrassing Room Mom Ever" (which is probably also accurate). I've been known to lead a class party in full costume (I mean, it was Pumpkin Day. Of course I was going to wear a pumpkin costume! That's a no-brainer.) I sing, I dance, I even tell funny jokes. Basically, I pretend I'm a talk show host and those little faces staring back at me are my adoring fans. I even like to give away prizes. Once, a teacher clipped on a hands-free mic to my shirt—total dream come true. Oh, and let's not forget the party where a handful of other amazing mother friends and I scheduled a petting zoo to visit the school playground—let's just say we may have had "World's Best Room Mom" trophies made for ourselves for that one . . .

This gumball machine craft was created with a classroom party in mind, but it's a great summer activity too. It's an inexpensive way to keep the kids busy, but it doesn't take so long that they lose patience, and it gives them something awesome to display at home.

INSTRUCTIONS

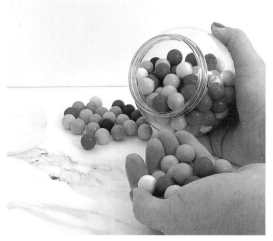

1 **Fill the globe.** Unscrew the snow globe lid and fill the empty globe with gumballs. Reattach the lid.

2 **Adhere the cup.** Adhere the snow globe lid onto the bottom of the plastic cup using a large dollop of hot glue.

3 **Prepare the dispenser.** Cut off the handle of the plastic spoon using a pair of sharp craft scissors, leaving about ½" (1.5cm) of the handle attached to the bowl of the spoon. This will serve as the faux gumball machine dispenser.

4 **Attach the dispenser.** Hot glue the cut spoon piece onto the plastic cup about an inch below the top, with the cut side up.

Continued on page 56

Keep an eye on your kiddo the first time they open their gumball machine for a treat. They need to flip it upside down to twist off the red cup and grab some gum. No one wants to pick up 100 gumballs off the floor.

5 **Attach a few gumballs.** Hot glue three gumballs to the dispenser.

6 **Attach a few more gumballs.** Hot glue more gumballs around the base of the snow globe.

TIP

When using hot glue in the classroom or at home with the kids, it's best to have a glue gun station: a table or desk at which an adult or responsible older child handles the glue gun and applies the piping hot glue for the younger kids as needed.

Vacation Travel

Traveling with eight kids and two dogs is certainly not for the faint of heart. As every mother in the history of ever has learned, when in an enclosed moving vehicle with children and pets, you *must* expect the unexpected. Preparation is key! Before we set out on any sort of long-distance adventure, I make sure I have all my bases covered in the event of a disaster. A sudden onslaught of motion sickness? I've got cleaning wipes, paper towels, and plastic bags for that. An uncontrollably snotty nose? No worries— we have loads of tissues and a bottle of children's decongestant. Need a trash can for all those dirty tissues and wipes? Pass back the plastic cereal box turned travel trash can. (These are actually the perfect size to hold a plastic shopping bag, and the sealed lid with the flip-top spout eliminates trash spills!)

In an attempt to start off the trip organized, I designate separate plastic tubs to hold all the supplies that may be necessary on our voyage away from home. I keep the emergency stocked storage bins up in the front of the van, close at hand to my seat, to ensure I can quickly grab and throw whatever is needed STAT to whoever requires it. Nothing makes a person move faster than the sound of a child gagging and retching from motion sickness in a vehicle! But preparation will help prevent everyone else from going green too.

MUST-PACK ITEMS

✓ Tissues
✓ Cleansing wipes
✓ Antibacterial wipes
✓ Plastic bags
✓ Band-Aids
✓ Easy and quick activities
✓ Water flavoring packets
✓ Individually wrapped snacks
✓ Reusable water bottles

I prep one bin for medicine and bodily functions and one bin for quick-deploy entertainment.

Caramel Corn Snack

INGREDIENTS

- 3 qts. (3 bags) popcorn, light or no butter, already popped
- ½ cup salted butter
- 1 cup brown sugar
- ¼ cup corn syrup
- ½ tsp. salt
- ½ tsp. baking soda
- 1 tsp. vanilla
- Cashews/party nuts (optional)

At times, it seems like the only way to truly relax and take a load off when the kids are little and the day is long is to put on a good family-friendly movie and eat some yummy popcorn. The bagged microwave stuff is great on its own, for sure, but if you want to take your popped snacking to the next level, this is the recipe you need! It's just the right amount of sweet and crunchy, making it totally addicting. A good friend shared this ingredient list with me, and I'm here to tell you, it's the absolute cream of the crop when it comes to gussying up your instant air-pop.

Fair warning, this is one totally addictive snack.

INSTRUCTIONS

1. Preheat oven to 250°F (120°C).
2. Place already-popped popcorn in a large, buttered pan. Keep warm in the oven.
3. Melt butter in a saucepan.
4. Stir in brown sugar, corn syrup, and salt. Bring to a boil while stirring constantly.
5. Next, slowly boil without stirring for 4–5 minutes to allow the sauce time to thicken.
6. Remove syrup mixture from heat and slowly stir in baking soda and vanilla.
7. Remove warmed popcorn from the oven and mix with syrup.
8. Add nuts if desired.
9. Spread popcorn back out on the pan and bake for 1 hour, stirring every 15–20 minutes.
10. Remove from oven, allow to cool, and break apart into bite-sized pieces.

Ice Cream Cone Garland

SUPPLIES

- 10 fillable plastic craft ornament balls— we used 2" (5cm) and 3" (8cm) balls
- White craft paper
- Hot glue
- Acrylic paint—we chose pastel sherbet colors: pearlescent pink, blue, cream, green, and orange
- Felt in coordinating colors
- 48" (122cm) length of white string
- Scissors

I've pretty much always been a "dessert first" kind of gal. Sometimes, when I'm feeling extra proud of my family (or after we've collectively survived a crazy hard week—ahem, I'm looking at you, virtual school!), I will loudly announce "Ice cream for dinner!" If you've never experienced an elephant stampede, the best course of action is to stop, drop, and roll. I know, we're not talking about fire, but the threat and the result is still the same: total devastation. And trust me when I tell you, do not get in between a gaggle of rambunctious children on their way to grab their ice cream bowls and get in line for their dinner scoops!

Seriously, though, breaking routine and having a backward kind of supper with dessert first (or even *only* dessert) is a great way to surprise the fam. Personally, I'm not too picky about what that dessert is, either. Cookies, cake, brownies, ice cream—I don't discriminate with my sweet tooth desires. But there's just something about summertime and ice cream that goes hand in hand like PB&J; like mac and cheese. Heck, even like a fine gas station wine and a block of Colby Jack cheese. They're just so right together. And there's no better way to commemorate summer than with an ice cream celebration! This garland brings the party on a string. Plus, you can leave it up the whole sunny season because it just makes you feel oh-so-cool!

TIP

Instead of making your own cones, you can use premade ice cream cone paper sleeves!

On a night when ice cream is for dinner, why not pull out all the stops and string an ice cream cone garland over the table?

INSTRUCTIONS

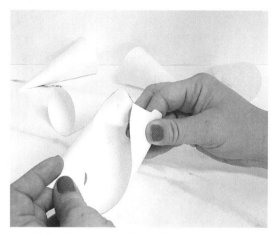

1 **Make the cones.** Cut white paper using a cone template to create your cones (see our cone template on page 156). Roll each cutout into a cone shape and apply a dab of hot glue to the exposed edge to hold the cone together.

2 **Squeeze in paint.** Generously squeeze acrylic paint inside each ornament ball, using about 1–2 tbsp. per ornament.

3 **Shake the ornament.** After securely closing the ornament, shake it until the inside is completely covered in paint. If necessary, drain excess paint back into the paint bottle. If there seems to be a lot of leftover paint, you may need to place the ornament upside down over a cup to drain it. Allow the ornament to completely dry.

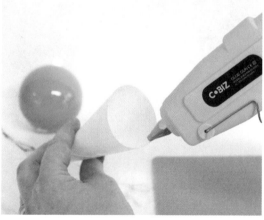

4 **Assemble the cone.** Attach the colored ball to the paper cone by hot gluing the bottom of the ball to the upper inside lip of the cone.

Continued on page 64

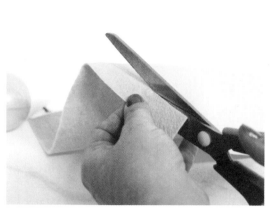

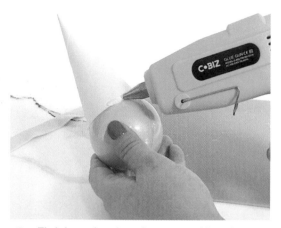

5 **Prep the felt.** Measure and cut felt into 1" x 12" (2.5 x 30.5cm) strips using colors that coordinate with the acrylic paint.

6 **Finish and string the cones.** Hot glue the strips in a ruffled fashion to the bottom circumference of each ball, right along the cone's edge. Run string through the tops of the ornament balls, knotting the string onto the hanger of each ornament to keep the ice cream cones from sliding around.

Birthday Party Craft

Need a fun and quick birthday party activity for your teen and her friends? How about tie-dying shoes? Grab some cheap, plain white tennies, colorful permanent markers, and rubbing alcohol. You may also want to tape up the rubber soles with painters' tape for a cleaner finish. Simply color your pattern or design on the shoes with the markers, apply the alcohol with a spray bottle or medicine dropper, and watch the artsy magic happen right before your eyes as the colors blend and bleed together into a crazy-cool tie-dyed look. Bonus: the girlies will all have matching shoes and a party favor to take home! In my humble opinion, it's not nearly as fun as sitting around your dining room table playing Heartthrob or Dream Phone with your girlfriends while jamming to your NKOTB cassette tape on the stereo, but it's a close second!

Homemade(ish) Dr. Cake

INGREDIENTS

- 1 box cake mix, any flavor
- 1 box instant pudding mix (3 oz.), any flavor
- 1 cup flour
- 1 cup sugar
- ¾ tsp. salt
- 1⅓ cups water
- ⅛ cup vegetable oil
- 2 tsp. vanilla
- 1 cup sour cream or Greek yogurt; if you're hardcore and goin' all milli-vanilli (I typically do), you can even use vanilla Greek yogurt
- 3 large eggs

I know, I know. You're wondering, "What the hey? Why the heck did she name this cake 'Dr.'?" Trust me, it's aptly named. See, it's been doctored up so much from the original box from whence it came, it's basically got a doctorate in the technical field of Homemade(ish). It's honestly an "anything goes" recipe that starts with a prepackaged mix and ends up tasting like a "stood in your kitchen all day and created this from scratch" recipe. You can stick with traditional flavors: chocolate cake and chocolate pudding, vanilla cake and vanilla pudding. Or mix it up and go off the rails: vanilla cake with lemon pudding for a zesty tang, vanilla cake with butterscotch pudding for a warm and creamy flavor, chocolate cake with banana cream pudding for a rich and decadent taste . . . you get the idea. It works as both a cake and a batch of cupcakes, to boot!

INSTRUCTIONS

1. Preheat oven to 325°F (163°C).
2. Grease and flour cake pans or cupcake tins. Keep in mind that the additional ingredients will increase the amount of batter you are making. I can easily fill three 6" (15cm) round cake pans, one huge sheet pan, or two 9" (23cm) round pans. You get a lot of cake with this recipe!
3. Mix all dry ingredients (cake mix, pudding mix, flour, sugar, salt) thoroughly.
4. Add wet ingredients (water, oil, vanilla, sour cream/yogurt, eggs) and beat well.
5. Pour batter into prepared pans, filling a bit more than halfway full.
6. Bake until cake is firm. Baking time varies based on pan size. Follow box directions. You may find that you need to increase your baking time depending on how full your pan is. 325°F (163°C) is a good temperature because it allows the cake to bake thoroughly without the worry of burning the top. The lower temperature and additional bake time will allow for a more even bake.

TIP

Dissolving 1 tsp. of instant coffee in water and adding it to a chocolate boxed cake mix will enhance the flavor and deliver a yummy, moist final result!

Book Pouch

SUPPLIES

- Hardcover book
- Pencil pouch in the right size to fit inside the book
- Utility knife
- Hot glue gun
- Ruler
- Permanent marker
- Scrap leather piece
- Sharp scissors

As a completely shameless literary nerd, I don't remember a time when reading wasn't a favorite pastime of mine. Even through my adolescence, Jane Austen and Charlotte Brontë were as much a part of my teenage angst as 90210 and VH1 were. While my peers were grudgingly reading their assigned English Lit books, I was nose deep in *The Last of the Mohicans* (because, obviously, I had finished my required reading early). To this day, I revere an opportunity to get lost in a book for hours on end. This doesn't really happen, because all these people in my home seem to think they need to eat three times a day and wear new outfits every morning . . . but a girl can dream, right?

My love of books has resulted in quite the compilation of hardcovers, softcovers, and pop-up books in our home library. It's a collection that I'm truly proud of. Not because we have first editions or rare copies, but because there are endless stories to be told and worlds to discover right in our very own dining room. Whenever I look at the shelves stuffed full of cockeyed, crooked, upside-down, backward, and randomly stacked books, I feel privileged to call those messy shelves mine. And I honestly think there's no better gift to give your children than the gift of a story.

So, when I came across someone selling a cardboard box full of colorful, vintage hardcover children's books a few blocks from our house (and the seller was practically giving them away), I was ecstatic. Like, "Kids! Drop everything you're doing and get in the van right now—I don't even care if you put on pants or shoes!" ecstatic. There were a couple of books that had double copies in the box. I sorted through the volumes and picked the ones with the fewest tears and dog-eared pages to keep for reading. I used the extra, more worn copies to create a couple of super cool book pouches. And even though my daughter looks way cuter with one at her side, I use mine as often as I can. If there was a "most fashionable way to carry your library card around" award, this would be the winner!

1 **Choose a good set of supplies.** Make sure that your pouch will fit inside the shape of the hardcover. It's best if the pouch is almost as big as the book.

2 **Remove the pages.** Use a utility knife to remove the pages of the book by cutting along the spine in the back and front.

3 **Check the spine.** This is what your hardcover should look like when you remove the paper pages—the hardcover binding should still be in one complete piece with a flexible spine.

4 **Attach the pouch spine.** Run hot glue along the outer spine of the pouch, opposite the zipper. Then press the pouch firmly to the inside spine of the book.

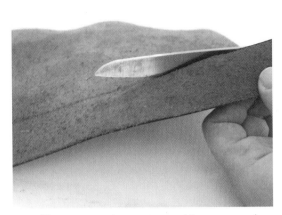

5 **Measure and cut straps.** Measure and mark two 1" x 12" (2.5 x 30.5cm) strips on the back side of the leather using a permanent marker. Using sharp scissors, cut out the strips.

6 **Attach the straps.** Hot glue both ends of one leather strip to the interior of the book's front cover and both ends of the other strip to the interior of the book's back cover.

7 **Glue one half.** Apply hot glue to one side of the pouch, then press it carefully against the inner cover, making sure to line everything up neatly with the spine.

8 **Glue the other half.** Repeat for the other side of the pouch and the other inner cover.

Lazy Susan Herb Planter

SUPPLIES

- Potted herbs
- 5½" (14cm) white plastic plant pots and saucers
- 14" (36cm) wooden lazy Susan
- Wool felt balls (polyester pom-pom balls work as well)
- Hot glue gun

Grow a few extra sprouts in some decorated pots to give as gifts.

Whether I've been barefoot and pregnant or just chubby and hungry, I've always loved being in my kitchen. That's not just because I've created a homey and vintage-shabby-grandma-style room that makes me happy simply sitting in it, but because I really do love to cook and bake for my family and friends. Full disclosure: I don't do fancy-schmancy meals. Uncomplicated, down-home recipes that require basic ingredients and are served buffet-style are more my family's palate (we're feeling gourmet when there's a few whole bay leaves floating around in our soup—ooh la la!).

But one thing I am completely adamant about as this household's resident Scullery Cook* is fresh herbs. There is an unmistakable difference between herbs that have been added to a meal freshly cut from the stem and herbs that are store-bought from a bottle. Don't get me wrong; I use a lot of herbs out of a bottle too. But I have a few potted herb plants that I make sure to always have on hand. Basil, parsley, and rosemary are three of my favorites due to their robust flavors, incredible aromas, and ease of keeping alive (the latter reason being the most important). This lazy Susan herb planter will for sure up the ante on your culinary skills! It is a perfect accompaniment to any kitchen countertop and allows easy sunlight rotation for herbs—something necessary for any window garden. Bonus: most big grocery stores sell planted herbs right in their produce departments!

*I find that my Mom jobs are much more bearable if I am awarded a pretentious title. For instance, while helping my homeschool kids with classwork, I request that they refer to me as "Professor Gambaccini." If I'm scrubbing the tub, I shall only turn my head for "Governess." Trust me, it helps. Try it.

TIP

The keys to a successful kitchen herb garden are sun, warmth, and water. Most herbs require 6–8 hours of sunlight, 60–70°F (15–21°C) temperatures, and infrequent, thorough waterings. You can dry your own herbs by placing the freshly picked leaves or seeds on a cookie sheet and baking on the lowest heat setting (less than 180°F or 82°C) for 2–4 hours or until the herbs crumble easily. Store dried herbs in a sandwich bag or an airtight food storage container, or freeze in ice cube trays filled with olive oil.

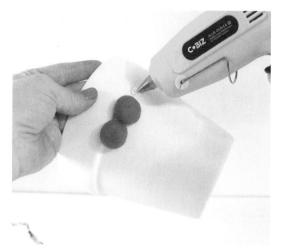

1 **Glue on the balls.** Hot glue the wool felt balls to the sides of the plant pots, one at a time.

2 **Continue gluing.** Continue gluing the balls to the pots until you are happy with the designs. Create different designs on each pot.

TIP

Instead of buying new, check your local secondhand stores for an inexpensive lazy Susan tray!

3 **Finish the setup.** Add the herbs and arrange the pots on the lazy Susan to make it easy to access and water each pot.

Homemade Bug Spray

I've always disliked spraying my kids with drugstore mosquito-repellent products. When I read the manufacturers' labels, it seems these sprays are full of way too much unknown junk, and the over-the-counter sprays tend to leave skin feeling sticky and gross. Not a good combination of feelings for anyone on hot, humid summer nights. So I decided to try my own hand at a more natural, homemade option.

I don't normally use essential oils for anything in my home other than to put in my cute diffuser that I absolutely love as a cover-up-the-baby-poop-smell air freshener. But I find making this bug spray to be a perfect reason to whip out all your essential oils!

I promise you that this DIY bug and mosquito repellent is clean and fresh, and it doesn't leave an oily residue. Plus, you can make it in less than 5 minutes. Just mix it all together in a spray bottle, and you're good to go! I make it in large batches to keep in the camper, and it lasts all season long!

INGREDIENTS

- ½ cup water
- ½ cup witch hazel
- 1 tbsp. rubbing alcohol or vodka
- 30 drops citronella essential oil
- 30 drops lemongrass essential oil
- 20 drops lavender essential oil
- 20 drops tea tree essential oil
- 20 drops eucalyptus essential oil
- 10 drops peppermint essential oil

Sunflower Wreath

SUPPLIES

- Large sheet of cardboard, at least 12" (30.5cm) square
- Hobby/craft knife
- 24" x 36" (61 x 91cm) piece of yellow felt in three different shades (this can include orange as the darkest shade)
- Sharp fabric scissors
- Forty ½" (1.5cm) brown pom-pom balls
- Paper plate
- 12" (30.5cm) length of twine
- Hot glue gun
- Handheld single-hole punch

TIP

Using a hammer and a nail or even simply jabbing a fine-tip pen or sharpened pencil through the cardboard would work in place of the hole punch.

I admit it: I'm a total sucker when it comes to a good door wreath. I can't help but have one for every holiday. I mean, if first impressions really matter, then your front door and how it's dressed would set the foundation for how a visiting first-time guest regards your home, right? Plus, I can't help but think that a coordinating door hanger for every season and celebration just screams to passersby, "Hey! We're pretty darn fun in here! You're probably going to want to be best friends with the lady of the house, 'cause she's cool!" And let me tell you, we are most definitely pretty darn fun up in this casa, and I am pretty ding-dong-dang cool if I do say so myself!

I mean, sure, you may occasionally hear yelling and fighting and arguing and lots of sounds that sound, well, not fun coming out the windows and walls. But what house with a bunch of kids in it doesn't have those noises permeating from the interior occasionally?

One thing is for certain: regardless of what's going on inside this place, I'll always have snacks and coffee (or wine, I'm not judgy) ready and waiting for anyone who wants to stop by and help me fold this mountain of towels in the laundry basket. Or at least just provide me some Big People conversation for a bit. And what better way to guarantee that your visitors feel all the welcoming love (and maybe ignore all the other not-so-good stuff) when they approach your door than by ensuring the first thing they see is something that reminds them of summer's best, of everything good and bright that the solstice has to offer? This sunflower wreath will welcome friends and visitors (and maybe even a few bees!) to your door in the best way possible—with the promise and color of warm, sunny, yellowy happiness.

This project is a great way to brighten a rainy day for both you and your neighbors.

INSTRUCTIONS

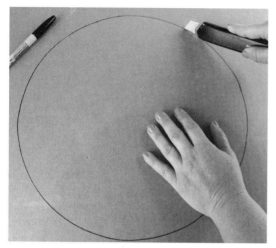

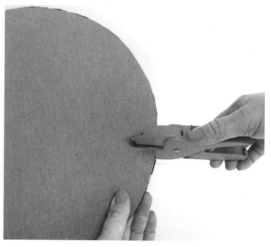

1 **Cut out a circle.** Trace and cut out a 12" (30.5cm) circle in the cardboard using a hobby/craft knife.

2 **Punch a hole.** Using the hole punch, punch a hole about 1" (2.5cm) from the rim of the circle.

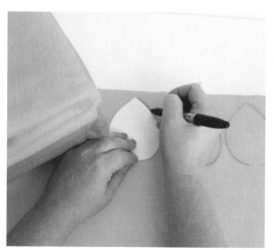

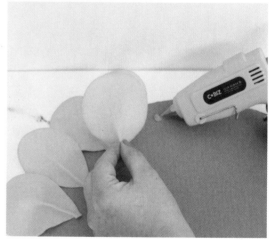

3 **Cut the petals.** Using the petal template on page 156, cut the following number of petals from the felt: 44 light yellow petals, 44 medium yellow petals, and 22 dark yellow/orange petals.

4 **Shape and glue the petals.** Starting with the lightest shade of yellow petals, crush each petal at the base as shown and hot glue it to the cardboard circle about 1" (2.5cm) from the outside edge so that the petal sticks out from the circle.

Continued on page 80

This wreath looks better the more petals you can pack in. Help kids grow their scissors skills while they help you cut all the petals.

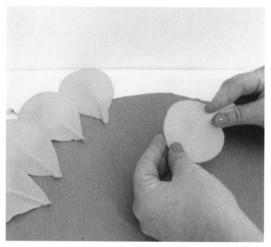

5 **Continue around the circle.** Continue working all the way around the circle, using 22 light yellow petals, and then start another row right inside the first using the same shade of yellow, using the other 22 petals.

6 **Use all the colors.** Start the third and fourth row using the medium shade of yellow, using 22 petals per row; once you've used up all those petals, finish with the darkest shade of yellow.

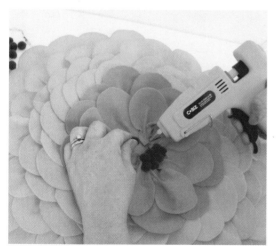

7 **Add the pom-poms.** Hot glue the pom-poms to the inside of the circle, one at a time.

8 **Add the twine.** Wrap and tie the twine through the hole for hanging.

S'mores Station

What's summer without camping, and what's camping without s'mores? One of my go-to sanity-saving schemes while out in the wilderness is taking the time to put together a S'mores Loading Station. Something you'll learn really quickly when camping with kids (other than the importance of knowing *exactly* how far it is to the nearest pit toilet) is how horrifyingly dangerous something as innocent as roasting marshmallows is. Take all the scalding-hot stainless-steel pokers getting whipped around through the air, narrowly missing eyes and other equally important body parts, and add the melted-marshmallow-is-about-to-fall-off-the-stick panicked run to the table for graham crackers, and you've got yourself a hazardous situation that could easily turn your vacation into something out of the Griswold family's memory album.

In my attempt to protect all my people's peepers (and in general keep the kids out of the ER), I started erecting a S'mores Loading Station at the picnic table. On a large plastic plate or platter, I break up all the graham crackers, separate all the chocolate squares, and open and dump all the marshmallows. I make sure I'm plopped at the end of the bench seat where all the hot pokers can be placed along the side edge of the table (sharp end down in the ground) until they are cooled and needed again. Serving as the official S'mores Steward, I take my position seriously, sandwiching melted 'mallows straight off the stick in between graham cracker squares and ensuring that those pesky kids with their sticky fingers don't steal all the chocolate bars!

S'more S'mores

INGREDIENTS

- 1 cup salted butter, softened
- 1½ cups sugar
- 2 tsp. vanilla
- 2 eggs
- 2⅔ cups flour
- 1½ cups graham crackers, coarsely crumbled
- 2 tsp. baking powder
- ½ tsp. salt
- Ten 1.5-oz. milk chocolate bars
- 6 cups miniature marshmallows

Nothing compares to a freshly-melted, made-over-the-campfire s'more. The ooey-gooey marshmallow with the melted chocolate and crunchy graham cracker is an infamously messy summertime snack. As a camping family, we've found that munching on s'mores is a vital and fundamental part of our evenings together around the fire. But did you know that there's a way to take this fireside favorite on the go in the form of a dish? Share these superbly sweet s'more s'mores at your next barbecue, potluck, or family reunion—everyone will love them and beg you for s'more!

INSTRUCTIONS

1. Preheat oven to 350°F (175°C) and grease a 9" x 13" (23 x 33cm) baking dish.
2. In a mixer, beat butter and sugar until well blended.
3. Add vanilla and egg, beating well.
4. In a separate bowl, mix flour, graham crackers, baking powder, and salt.
5. Add dry ingredients to butter mixture, beating until blended.
6. Divide dough in half. Spread one half in an even layer in the dish and bake for 15 minutes.
7. Unwrap chocolate bars and arrange the squares on top of baked crumb layer, breaking pieces as needed to fit.
8. Sprinkle marshmallows over the chocolate.
9. Scatter chunks of the remaining dough over the marshmallows, forming a top layer.
10. Bake for 10–15 minutes or until lightly browned.
11. Allow to cool completely before serving.

Sometimes you just need to accept that something ooey-gooey is going to be messy. I'll take a great memory over a clean kid any day.

This is the perfect way to take everyone's fireside favorite on the go in the form of a dish!

PARTY OF ONE & PICKY EATERS

FAVORITES FOR SINGLE KIDS

Most of our activities are done together as a big ol' family. But sometimes it really is nice to break apart and spend a little one-on-one time with each of the kiddos. In truth, Edward and I need that QT as much as they do! I love to spend time with my kids while teaching them life skills in the kitchen or making a craft "just because." Having a smaller crew while we create also means I can tailor the project to suit them and their interests. For instance, the older the child, the more willing I am to pull out the hot glue and, if I'm in a *really* good mood, maybe even those wretched glitter bottles!

That's why, in this section, you'll find crafts and activities that are better suited to single kids and that require a little more focus and attention from you as a parent. Trust me, the rewards are worth it! Plus, the recipes will please the palate of even the pickiest of eaters, so you can feed your kids and have fun together, too.

Embellished Umbrella
(page 14)

Carrot Cake
(page 38)

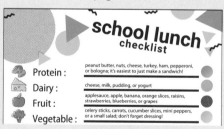

school lunch checklist

Protein : peanut butter, nuts, cheese, turkey, ham, pepperoni, or bologna; it's easiest to just make a sandwich!

Dairy : cheese, milk, pudding, or yogurt

Fruit : applesauce, apple, banana, orange slices, raisins, strawberries, blueberries, or grapes

Vegetable : celery sticks, carrots, cucumber slices, mini peppers, or a small salad; don't forget dressing!

Packed Lunches
(page 91)

Celebration Chocolate Chip Cookies
(page 154)

Book Pouch
(page 68)

Cozy Coaster
(page 124)

Candy Corn Buttons
(page 100)

BIRTHDAY PARTIES & SPECIAL TREATS

GREAT FOR BIRTHDAY BASHES, SLUMBER PARTIES, AND OTHER CELEBRATIONS

For Edward and I, hosting birthday parties, get-togethers, or any kind of guests is no big deal—we're used to dealing with the chaos and mess that comes with having a bunch of people in the home. So, when you really want to amp the fun up to the next level, get the kids involved in these crafts, activities, and recipes. They're perfect for large, energetic groups, scaling up easily, and making just enough mess to know that you're having a good time. Plus, saving them for special occasions will only make them sweeter!

Whenever you whip out these projects and tasty treats, follow some other tried-and-true party advice that Edward and I have learned along the way: make sure there's a trash bag in every entertaining area; switch out the bathroom hand towels for paper towels; don't stress over the menu (people love all free food); and always take a minute to greet every guest, no matter how hectic things are.

Caramel Corn Snack
(page 58)

Ice Cream Cone Garland
(page 60)

Homemade(ish) Dr. Cake
(page 66)

Best Ever Sugar Cookies
(page 148)

Sidewalk Popsicle Chalk
(page 40)

Bubblegum Machine
(page 52)

Birthday Party Craft
(page 65)

CHAPTER 3

Fall-ing Back into Routine

When Edward built our front porch, we talked about how wonderful it would be to be able to relax on the swing while watching the kids play in the yard and how we couldn't wait to sit outside during rain showers and see the sky change. While all of this was true, as everyone knows that the main purpose of a front porch is intentional slow living, I was also secretly ecstatic at the thought of having another area to decorate. I'm quite certain this "secret" of mine was no surprise to Edward, as he knows me better than anyone on the planet, but I'd like to think I did a good job masking my true motivation for the extensive exterior renovation.

As soon as the final floorboard was in place, I started creating a front porch that was as equally as inviting as the interior of my home—an extension of the inside, really. We use the porch so much during the warmer months of the year that it's essentially additional living space. Need a break from the craziness going on inside the house? Head to the front porch. Need silence to make an important phone call? Go on out to the porch. Need to eat therapy ice cream in private without little people finding you and expecting you to share? The front porch is the place to be. I'm pretty sure if my fall scarecrows could talk, they'd tell you that life is better on the porch!

As the days start to get shorter and colder, we still love using the porch for hanging out on the nicer days and—of course—to welcome the world with our fall display.

Most of our seasonal décor gets stored in heavy plastic bins when not in use. For bulkier items like our scarecrows and plastic pumpkins, I skip the bins and go straight for the trash bags—plus, the bags are easier to carry up the steps into the storage attic!

Candy Apples (Nonedible)

SUPPLIES

- Faux apples
- Popsicle sticks
- Light brown or toffee acrylic paint
- White craft glue
- Small bowl
- Foam paintbrush (optional)
- Corncob bedding
- Clear spray topcoat (gloss finish)
- Twine

TIP

For an additional autumn touch, add a few drops of apple-scented fragrance oil around each candy apple for a warm and authentic smell.

I find myself perusing the aisles of our local dollar store every chance I get. Mostly it's just an excuse to get out of the house all by my lonesome for the purpose of regrouping what's left of my brain balance, but I also like to see what's new on the shelves. I find the store to be a magically cheap enigma where everything is a buck and you never know what new surprises are going to appear around the next corner. While my love for thrifty shopping is no secret, I cannot tell you how many times I've come home with my shopping haul only to have Edward say, "What are you going to do with that?" or "What are your plans for those?"

See, that's the rub. Most of the time I have no stinkin' clue. I see something that looks like something I may use sometime, and I bring it home. Now, I understand this isn't the best plan of action. But it's simply the way my creative brain works, and therefore it's all I've got to work with. And because every jolly item is just four quarters worth of merry-making, I have a bit more leeway budget-wise.

Take these apples, for example. They were just so cute that I couldn't walk by without dropping a handful of red and shiny faux fruits into my cart, even though I didn't have a solid plan for them. But in typical me fashion, a few weeks later, I experienced an "aha" moment of purpose regarding those sweet little apples. I envisioned candy apples in the kitchen to give us some majorly sweet and nutty fall vibes. Voila! Just like that, my dollar store shopping cycle was complete.

INSTRUCTIONS

1 **Insert Popsicle sticks.** Gently push a Popsicle stick into the top of each apple near the stem.

2 **Mix paint and white glue.** Mix 1 cup of paint and 1 cup of white glue in a medium-sized plastic bowl. Stir well.

3 **Dip the apple.** Holding onto the stick, dip each apple into the paint/glue mixture until it has the desired coverage. If necessary, use a foam paintbrush or spoon to help drip the paint over the apple.

4 **Decorate the apple.** Sprinkle the corncob bedding around the painted sections of each apple. Allow to fully dry.

5 **Add a protective coat.** Spray a coat of clear protective topcoat over the apples in a well-ventilated area, preferably outdoors.

6 **Add a bow.** Once the clear coat is dry to the touch, tie a length of twine into a bow around each Popsicle stick.

Packed Lunches

If your kiddos are older and want to be a bit more independent (or Mama is just plain flippin' tired), allowing them to pack their own lunches is always a good place to start. But it's probably best not to let the kids go all willy-nilly on their own in the kitchen without a bit of food prep supervision in the beginning. You never quite know what they'll pack. Trust me, I volunteered in the school cafeteria for years, and I always knew which kid made his or her own lunch with no adult guidance—I'm pretty sure Mom's frozen margarita Popsicle pouch will never be considered a proper substitute for a yogurt tube (just sayin'). I created a school lunch checklist to assist my kids in packing proper lunches. I have this sucker taped right inside the pantry door to make it easy to see and hard to miss. And, surprisingly enough, they reference it often when putting together their midday meals.

I also have the kids pack whatever they didn't finish that day at school right back into their lunch bags. This not only helps cut down on food waste (the dry, non-refrigerated goods can be reused if not open) but also gives me an idea of what they are eating. Are they packing too much? Too little? Is there something in there that they don't really care for that I should quit buying at the store? By seeing their lunch boxes after they've eaten, I have a better idea of what lunchtime is like when I'm not there.

You can photocopy this checklist for your own use on page 157; if you want to change any of the categories, just white them out and add your own!

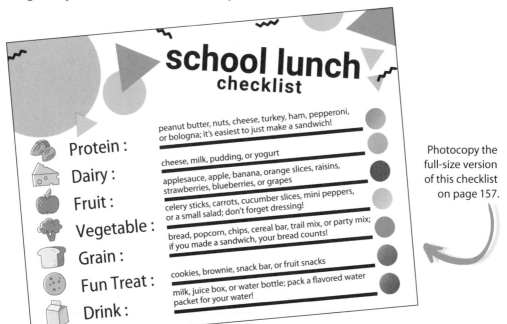

school lunch
checklist

Protein : peanut butter, nuts, cheese, turkey, ham, pepperoni, or bologna; it's easiest to just make a sandwich!

Dairy : cheese, milk, pudding, or yogurt

Fruit : applesauce, apple, banana, orange slices, raisins, strawberries, blueberries, or grapes

Vegetable : celery sticks, carrots, cucumber slices, mini peppers, or a small salad; don't forget dressing!

Grain : bread, popcorn, chips, cereal bar, trail mix, or party mix; if you made a sandwich, your bread counts!

Fun Treat : cookies, brownie, snack bar, or fruit snacks

Drink : milk, juice box, or water bottle; pack a flavored water packet for your water!

Photocopy the full-size version of this checklist on page 157.

Homemade Applesauce

INGREDIENTS

- 8 medium apples, peeled and cored
- 1½ cups water
- ½ cup white sugar
- 1 tsp. cinnamon
- 1 tsp. vanilla extract (the secret ingredient!)

INSTRUCTIONS

1. Mix all ingredients together in a saucepan.
2. Cover and cook over medium heat for 20–30 minutes or until apples are soft.
3. Mash with a potato masher, a fork, or an immersion blender until desired consistency.

Most normal households consider "grocery staples" to be items like eggs, bread, milk, cheese, and butter. Don't get me wrong; we use an absurd amount of said foodstuffs in our kitchen. But for my crazy-big fam, we have a few more crucial additions to the shopping list of necessary grub. For instance, ketchup. I dread the day we're serving up a big platter of French fries only to find out that the ketchup bottle had been put back in the fridge empty. And I'm not sure we could even "lunch" without hazelnut spread. Oh, and don't forget the esteemed creamy peanut butter—the perfect snack-on-a-spoon when you don't know what the heck else to stuff in your face.

But there is one thing that really throws us for a loop when we discover there's no backup jars on the pantry shelves, one element of sustenance that pretty much compliments any meal, one sauce that can be a side, a condiment, or a dessert, the king of all dinnertime fruits: applesauce.

Sometimes while my kiddos are slurping a spoonful of the sweet stuff, I can't help but reminisce a bit. Growing up, our family dinner table was a charcuterie board of condiments and side dishes. The salad dressing selection my mama put out every evening could rival even the best restaurant buffet. And there was always plenty of warm cinnamon applesauce and cottage cheese. My homemade applesauce recipe is a sort of nostalgic reminder of my childhood suppers past—it brings all the warm and fuzzies, makes your kitchen smell amazeballs, and can be whipped up last minute. I think we owe Johnny Appleseed big time!

TIP

For a smoother, less chunky applesauce, add ⅛ cup of water to the saucepan while cooking.

My homemade applesauce recipe is a nostalgic reminder of my childhood suppers past.

Jack-o'-Lantern Candy Holder

SUPPLIES

- 13" (33cm) carvable foam pumpkin
- Pencil
- Utility knife
- Hot glue
- 5" x 5" (13 x 13cm) piece of white felt
- Black marker
- Sharp scissors
- Battery-operated LED lights
- Spare length of wire or string
- Adhesive-backed hook-and-loop tape

TIP

The mouth needs to be a fairly wide opening to allow room for little hands to grab the candy. My pumpkin's mouth is approximately 4" x 7" (10 x 18cm).

I'm not sure which part of Halloween all my small monsters love more—the candy, the decorations, the not-so-scary movies, hearing "Thriller" on the radio in the van, or the fun costumes. Even as an adult, I still think dressing up in a costume is entertaining! Thanks to my hard-earned Mom Bod that accompanies my original everyday exhausted, just-rolled-out-of-bed look (not at all to be confused with the actually good-looking tousled beach waves you see in glamour magazines), I've never been one to try risqué costumes. My MO is more of an old crone ensemble. Did you know "mom" is actually the moniker for "witch"? OK, it's actually not. But I'm pretty sure my kids think it is, at least a few days out of every month. Frankly, I've always felt a sort of kinship to those heavily eye-shadowed Sanderson sisters from *Hocus Pocus*. I guess it's why I feel so comfortable dressing as a witch one night every year to take my crew trick-or-treating. Something about it just feels so *right*.

You want to know what else feels so right just for the night of October 31st? Eating way too much candy. It's pretty much a traditional requirement of the celebration. And I can't think of a more spooktacular way to display all those fun-sized candy bars and serve all those grubby little hands than with a pumpkin candy holder!

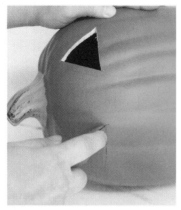

1 **Draw the face.** Draw out your jack-o'-lantern face and trace around the stem at the top of the pumpkin using a pencil.

2 **Cut out the features.** Using a utility knife, cut out the eyes, nose, and mouth as well as the stem from the top of the pumpkin, just like you would for a real pumpkin. Don't include teeth in the mouth—just cut the mouth outline.

3 **Draw the teeth.** Draw four large, square-shaped teeth on white felt with a black marker. Each tooth should be approximately 1" x 3" (2.5 x 8cm).

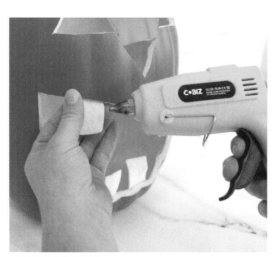

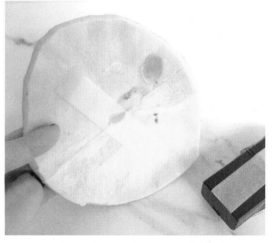

4 **Attach the teeth.** Using the hot glue gun, glue one tooth at a time to the interior of the pumpkin, making sure the black outline from the marker is not facing out.

5 **Attach the lights.** Wrap the lights into a bundle and secure using wire or string, then attach the bundle to the underside of the stem piece using adhesive-backed hook-and-loop tape, making sure you have easy access to the on/off switch on the battery box.

Pumpkin Saver

Did you know there is a way to prolong the life of your carved pumpkins and prevent that nasty, rotted bottom that sinks down onto the front porch stoop and leaves a stain for months? It's just an easy extra step that keeps your jack-o'-lantern looking fresh. Fill a large plastic container or bucket with approximately 3 gallons (11L) of cold water and mix in 3 tsp. (45mL) of liquid bleach. Drop the carved or whole pumpkin into the water, making sure to hold the pumpkin down, as it will want to float. Keep the pumpkin in the solution for at least two minutes. Allow the pumpkin to fully air dry.

Dinner in a Pumpkin

INGREDIENTS

- 1 pumpkin, small enough to fit in your oven (see step 1)
- 1 lb. boneless, skinless chicken breasts
- 1 tsp. garlic salt
- Salt and pepper
- ½ cup chopped carrots
- 1 can corn (15 oz.)
- 1 can peas (15 oz.)
- 2 tbsp. salted butter
- 2 tbsp. cream cheese
- 1½ cups instant white rice
- 1 cup water
- 1 cup cheddar cheese, shredded

All Hallows' Eve food fact: Did you know you could make a casserole in a pumpkin? I know what you're thinking: "Food in a pumpkin? You've got to be *jack-o'-lantern-in'* me around!" Nope—I swear to *gourd* this is a real thing. And it's totally awesome, my Halloween-loving friends. Dinner in a pumpkin is my go-to trick-or-treat-night meal. Jam-packed with veggies, it makes it a bit easier to let the costumed kids loose in the land of sugar knowing they've ingested some healthy stuff first.

Before we hop into the nitty-gritty of this ghoulishly delightful casserole recipe, I need to point out that there are actually two ways to make this meal. The first is for those who want the pumpkin look at dinner, but not the pumpkin taste. The second is for those pumpkin-lovin' peeps that can't get enough of the orange stuff this season and want to scoop up that baked goodness on the inside right along with the filling. Make sure you are following the proper recipe instructions for your pumpkin preference!

INSTRUCTIONS

1. Preheat oven to 350°F (175°C). The pumpkin will need to be placed on the lowest rack, so you will most likely need to remove the top rack from your oven for the pumpkin to fit, lid and all. Measure your maximum space, and make sure you buy a pumpkin that will fit.
2. Cut the top off the pumpkin and set aside. Make sure the opening is wide enough to allow ample room for you to spoon the casserole out.
3. Remove the seeds and insides of the pumpkin. You can carve a face on your pumpkin but, if you do, make sure to line that side with tinfoil so the casserole stays inside. Place the pumpkin sitting up on a foil-covered baking sheet.
4. Cook chicken, garlic salt, and salt and pepper together in a large skillet sprayed with cooking spray until evenly browned. Then shred the cooked chicken. For even faster prep, use cooked rotisserie chicken, de-skinned and shredded, instead.

There are two ways to make this meal, one for pumpkin lovers and one for the pumpkin ambivalent!

5. Add veggies, butter, and cream cheese. Continue to stir, keeping the pan over low heat, until thoroughly mixed.

6. Remove from stove. Stir in rice and water.

7. If you are NOT planning on baking the pumpkin, continue to heat the rice and water until the rice is fully cooked. Line the pumpkin with tinfoil and pour the cooked casserole into the pumpkin, then sprinkle shredded cheddar cheese generously on top. Serve immediately.

8. If you ARE planning to bake the pumpkin, pour the casserole into the gutted pumpkin, place the lid back on top, and bake for 90 minutes on the lowest rack in the oven.

9. Remove from the oven and sprinkle generously with shredded cheddar cheese. Let sit for 10 minutes or until cheese is melted.

10. Serve the pumpkin on a baking sheet, as it will be very soft and break easily after baking.

Candy Corn Buttons

SUPPLIES

- 2 oz. orange oven-bake clay
- 2 oz. yellow oven-bake clay
- 2 oz. white oven-bake clay
- Wax paper
- Baking sheet
- Baby wipes
- Triangle-shaped mini cookie cutter three-piece nesting set
- Mini rolling pin or fondant roller

These buttons are as easy to remove as they are to add when you're ready to pass this shirt down to the next child who might not be a fan.

I'm a bona fide thrift-store enthusiast. I love the thrill of the pre-owned hunt. As a matter of fact, many of my most favorite pieces of furniture and holiday decorations were purchased secondhand. Sometimes, I'm so proud of my cheapo skills that I can't help but shout it out to the world—or at least to my little cul-de-sac street. Take my $5 oriental rug set that is absolute perfection on my porch in the summer. You best believe anyone and everyone I spoke to for the two weeks after that purchase knew exactly how many quarters I splurged on those bad boys!

But here's the caveat: thrift shopping is a game of chance. You must be willing to walk out empty-handed but undefeated. You've got to go in those doors with high hopes and low expectations (come on, we've all been in that mindset *cough* *trendy diets* *cough*). If you do have a specific item you're on the prowl for, it may take several visits and even multiple stores before you find it, but eventually, you *will* find it. And it'll be downright thrilling when you do, my cheapskate friend.

But I don't just thrift for lamps and mini Christmas trees. Keeping a small, constantly growing army in right-sized pants is pricey. Even the older kids understand the significant difference between buying used and getting an armful of outfits versus buying new and getting only a few pieces. And the one thing I always keep an eye out for on those racks of secondhand goodness is solid-colored shirts. A cartoon character or boy band may not be as popular in five years when the next kiddo is in that particular clothing size, but a plain shirt never goes out of style. A simple top can be dressed up with a cute cardigan or worn with a pair of sweats for a lazy Saturday. You can even take those plain shirts to the next level by adding some handmade buttons—just like we did with these candy corn buttons.

Can you say Cute. As. A. Button? Plus, you get to play with clay. And I don't care how old you are, playing with clay will never not be fun!

It's easy to score solid-colored shirts at the thrift store for cheap! You can personalize each shirt to the kid who is going to wear it.

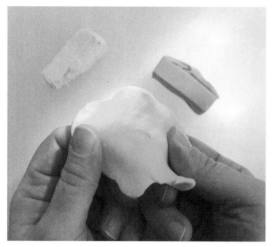

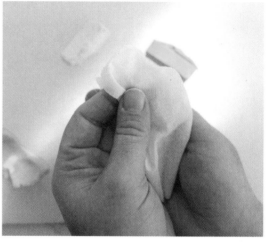

1 **Condition the clay.** Cover your workspace with wax paper (colored clay can bleed onto surfaces and countertops). Working with one-quarter of each block at a time, condition each clay piece by rolling the clay into a ball, flattening it out into a pancake shape, and repeating until the clay is warm and pliable. Conditioning will prevent any cracking that may occur during baking.

2 **Wipe hands between colors.** Make sure to wipe your hands thoroughly with a baby wipe every time you switch between colors to prevent color transfer.

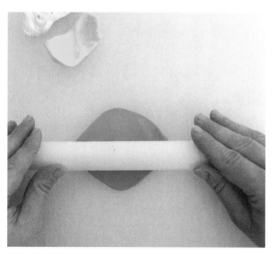

3 **Roll the orange clay.** Using the rolling pin, roll the orange clay until it is about ¼" (0.5cm) thick.

TIPS

✓ A little bit of clay goes a long way. Make sure to seal any leftover clay in resealable lunch baggies (with colors separated) to keep it fresh for your next project.

✓ In place of the mini triangle cutters, you could freehand cut your triangles using a hobby/craft knife or clay cutting tool and a bit of patience.

✓ When necessary, wash the shirts as directed on the laundry care tag. Oven-bake clay is machine washable!

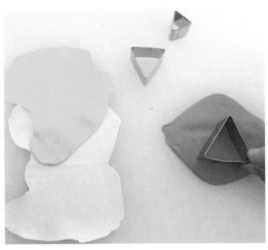

4 **Cut out the shape.** Taking the largest of the three triangle cutters, cut out the first shape and set it, as well as the leftover orange clay, aside.

5 **Repeat with the yellow clay.** Wipe down your workspace with a baby wipe and repeat steps 3 and 4 with the yellow clay, but use the medium-sized triangle cutter instead of the largest.

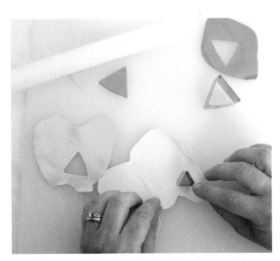

6 **Repeat with the white clay.** Repeat the process with the white clay, but use the smallest triangle cutter.

7 **Assemble the shape.** Lay the yellow triangle on top of the orange, then place the white triangle on top of the yellow, making sure the edges all line up. Using the bottom of a colored pencil or the eraser of a pencil, make an indent in the center of the yellow portion of the candy corn. This makes a depression for the thread to lie in, preventing it from getting worn.

8 **Add buttonholes.** With a nail head or sewing needle, push two buttonholes into the circular indentation.

9 **Prep for baking.** Make the rest of the buttons. Then preheat the oven to 275°F (135°C). Carefully transfer the buttons to a wax-paper-covered baking sheet.

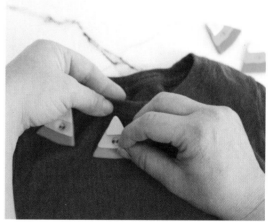

10 **Bake.** Place the baking pan in the oven on the middle rack and bake for 15 minutes. Remove the pan from the oven and allow the buttons to cool completely before handling them, about 15 minutes.

11 **Sew the buttons.** Sew the buttons to a clean purple, black, or white shirt along the collar. You can use any shirt color you like, but these colors go well with the candy corn and are quite Halloween-y!

Fancy Crust

In this bougie Insta-Pin world we're living in, we seem to feel more pressured than ever to present our families and friends with dishes and entrees worthy of a magazine photo shoot. But the hard truth is, ain't nobody got time for that. Fancy piecrusts just aren't a priority for most of us busy moms. I've often told my kids, "It's not what it looks like, it's what it tastes like that matters," regarding meals and dishes I've made. That's code for: "I totes screwed this up on the outside, but I *think* I mixed the ingredients right on the inside, so we should be good to eat it."

If Martha Stewart isn't your spirit animal and you find that you can't flute, braid, or latticework your piecrust, there's another way to make pies look ah-may-zing without all the sweat and tears. After all, anyone can use a cookie cutter! Starting with a mini cutter (I prefer fun, seasonally appropriate cutters in multiple coordinating shapes), simply cut out shapes from the rolled-out pie crust. You can create a unique pie border or fill the whole gosh darn top with the cutout pieces! You will want to cover your crust with tinfoil to prevent the edges of the cutouts from over-browning in the oven!

Use this tip when you're baking up the recipes on the following pages!

All-Butter Piecrust

INGREDIENTS

- 2½ cups flour
- 2 tbsp. sugar
- 1 cup cold salted butter, cubed
- ½ cup ice water

Here's a little life lesson for you, friends. Life may let you down. People may let you down. But this all-butter piecrust? It will never let you down. The ingredients are simple, the prep work is easy, and the result is delish. Whether you're making a hearty potpie or a sweet fruit pie, this crust is really all you'll ever need. I mean, the main ingredient is butter, so it's got to be good, right?

Note: You'll need two metal pie pans to make this recipe. Why metal? Because this is an all-butter crust, it needs to be frozen before baking to keep the pie shape. The extreme temperature change from freezer to oven could cause glass to shatter.

TIP

This recipe makes two regular-sized round piecrusts (top and bottom). But, if you are making a slab pie (in a large rectangular pan), this recipe will make just one slab piecrust.

INSTRUCTIONS

1. In a stand mixer, or by hand with a pastry cutter if you're old-school, blend flour and sugar together.
2. Add butter. Mix until the butter chunks are no bigger than blueberries.
3. Add ice water and mix until a dough ball forms.
4. Remove ball from bowl and cut in half. Flatten into two large pancake-shaped dough discs.
5. Flour counter and roll out each dough disc a few inches larger than the metal pie pans you are using. (The pans must be metal—see note above.)
6. Butter each pan and line the pans with the pie dough. Tuck under the edges evenly and beautify, aka crimp, them.
7. Place the pie shells into the freezer for at least an hour before baking, but preferably overnight.
8. When you are ready to bake your pie, fill the frozen crust and bake immediately—do not thaw the crust.
9. Preheat oven to 400°F (205°C). After 15 minutes, reduce oven to 375°F (190°C) and bake according to your recipe. Starting out with a very hot oven helps keep the shape of your crimping or decorative edge.

Perfectly Perfect Apple Pie

INGREDIENTS

- All-Butter Piecrust (recipe on page 106)
- 6 cups peeled and sliced apples (4-5 large apples)
- 1 tbsp. lemon juice
- ½ cup sugar
- ¼ cup brown sugar
- 1 tbsp. cornstarch
- ½ tsp. ground cinnamon
- ¼ tsp. ground nutmeg

TIP

This recipe freezes very well. If you pick a bunch of fresh apples in the fall, you can make extra batches to freeze and use throughout the winter.

An unbelievable truth: I never liked fruit pie until I started making my own.

I know, I know—cringey fact. The words seem blasphemous to even type out, let alone say out loud. Once I perfected my all-butter piecrust recipe and proceeded to move on to create a filling that would aid in the extinguishment of my pie scorn, then and only then did I change my tune to one of sweet pie love songs. I just know you'll enjoy my apple pie recipe too. This pie takes all the goodness of fresh, crunchy apples and combines a sweet and spicy mix to create a totally scrumptious filling for fall.

INSTRUCTIONS

1. Coat peeled and sliced apples with lemon juice.
2. In a large bowl, toss apples with sugars, cornstarch, cinnamon, and nutmeg using a large spoon.
3. Preheat oven to 400°F (205°C).
4. With your prepared and frozen All-Butter Piecrust ready to go in your pie pan, add apple and sugar mixture.
5. Decorate top of pie with cutout shapes for a fancier finished product (see Bright Idea on page 105).
6. Cover top of pie with tinfoil.
7. Lower oven temperature to 375°F (190°C).
8. Place pie in oven and bake for 50 minutes or until crust is golden brown.

Pumpkin Pie Garland

SUPPLIES

- Two 8" x 8" x 1" (20 x 20 x 2.5cm) Styrofoam craft circles/discs
- ½ yard (0.5m) orange felt
- ½ yard (0.5m) tan felt
- Hot glue gun
- White yarn
- ¾" (2cm) Styrofoam craft balls
- Twine
- Fabric scissors
- Pinking shears
- Woodburning tool or sharp hobby/craft knife

Man, I love me some Thanksgiving. I have so much fondness in my heart for the classic stuffed bird and all his side dishes that it was our wedding reception meal (Turkey and stuffing. Mashed potatoes and gravy. Beans and corn. Rolls and butter. The whole gosh darn shebang!). Plus, it's the one holiday that I look forward to wearing my elastic-waisted, super stretchy party pants to dinner at sweet Aunt Jane's house, because I know for a flat-out fact that I'm going to overindulge and *gobble* (sorry, mom joke) up everything in sight! And Edward's aunt certainly makes sure there's a cornucopia of sweet and salty treats for us to sample before, during, and after the traditional turkey and stuffing platter. Plus, the fact that it also happens to be one of the few meals a year that I don't have to cook makes me adore this celebration of eating that much more.

Of course, this includes those oh-so-sweet triangle-shaped slices of pumpkin-y heaven. Yep—you know I'm talking about pie. I have some pretty strong *fillings* about pie (am I on a joke roll, or what?). As an homage to the ultimate Thanksgiving Day dessert, I've created this pumpkin pie garland to hang over your mantle or across your holiday dessert table. But no matter where you put it, it'll leave you and your dinner guests dreaming of warm homemade crusts, overflowing fillings, and great dollops of whipped cream.

TIP

If you don't have a woodburning tool, a sharp hobby/craft knife will do the job, but it will require multiple cuts to get through the foam and will be quite messy. A woodburning tool cuts through the Styrofoam like butter.

INSTRUCTIONS

1 **Trace and cut the circles.** Trace the Styrofoam circle onto the orange felt twice. Using sharp fabric scissors, cut out the two felt circles.

2 **Draw the pie slices.** Draw out the pie slices on the felt circles using a ruler and marker, dividing each circle into four or six equal "slices." Cut all the slices apart.

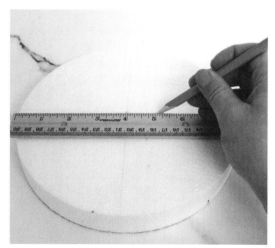

3 **Mark the Styrofoam.** Mark the same pie slices into the Styrofoam circles to match the felt slices.

4 **Cut the foam circles.** With a woodburning tool set on the lowest setting (or a hobby/craft knife), cut the foam circles on the marked lines to divide them into slices.

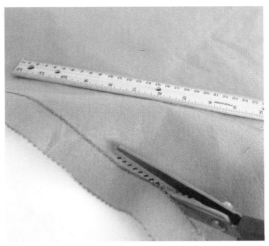

5 **Cut orange felt strips.** Cut eight 12" x 1" (30.5 x 2.5cm) strips from the orange felt using fabric scissors. These will be the sides of the pie.

6 **Cut tan felt strips.** Cut twelve 12" x 1" (30.5 x 2.5cm) strips from the tan felt using pinking shears. These will be the crust.

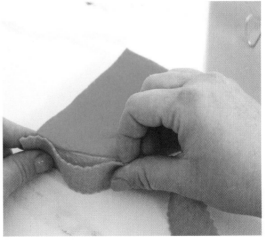

7 **Glue the orange slices.** With the hot glue gun set on the lowest setting, glue the orange felt slices to the top of the Styrofoam slices. Make sure to glue them marker side down.

8 **Glue the tan strips.** Hot glue the tan strips around the back of each pie slice for the crust.

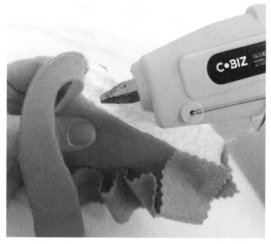

9 **Glue the orange strips.** Next, hot glue the orange strips around the sides of the pie slices for the filling.

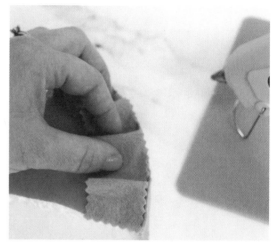

10 **Add a decorative top crust.** Trim any extra felt hanging off the slices using your scissors. To add a decorative top crust, take the remaining tan strips and hot glue one on the top of each slice, crimping the strip into a wavy pattern.

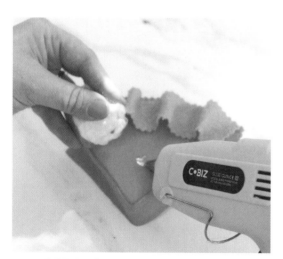

11 **Add the Styrofoam balls.** For the whipped cream, wrap each Styrofoam ball using a piece of white yarn 12" (30.5cm) long. Hot glue a ball to the top of each slice.

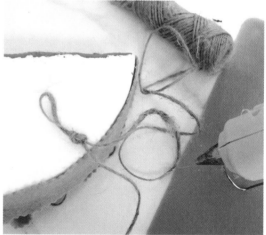

12 **Assemble the garland.** Hot glue twine to the back of each pie piece along the top to combine all the pieces into a garland you can hang.

Game Day

A recycled plastic cookie jar serves as the catchall for misplaced toys and game parts.

Nothing brings out my family's competitive temperament quite like a classic board game. Whenever we break out those cardboard boxes of fun, I know we're in for a whole bunch of good old-fashioned quality family bonding time. The next hour is typically full of giggles and lots of snacks and spilled drinks. And, if I'm being honest, a handful of pouting bouts mixed with a few tears. It's just plain hard for little ones to grasp the art of how not to be a sore loser. And for kids of all ages, it's hard to practice being a good winner. After all the stress and frustration from playing the game, that in-your-face victory attitude seems to sneak up on even the most easygoing kid, leaving the ones suffering defeat even more sour. In our house, our number one gaming rule is: Winner Cleans Up. Not only does it solve the problem of who is responsible for putting all the game pieces away, it also softens the blow for the losers and makes for a bit humbler of a champion. It's a win-win, really!

No matter which kid is conducting cleanup duty, without a doubt there will be at least three pieces, two cards, and the instruction booklet left out. This is why we have a container for lost toys. It's a recycled plastic cookie jar that is now the home of all the misplaced toy and game parts that we've found under the refrigerator, at the bottom of the toy box, or in the couch cushions. All those random pieces get tossed into the lost toys jar. That way, the next time we're playing the memory game and realize we are four cards short, we know just where to look!

Thanksgiving Casserole

"What's for dinner?"

This seemingly innocent query is one that I am asked at least seven times every night—not even joking, people. Typically, it's even more than that, since one or two of the kids ask this same gosh darn question multiple times while I'm in the kitchen preparing supper. Just writing about our nightly Q&A session makes me want to lose what's left of my ever-lovin' mind. There are days that I don't even have a proper title for what I'm cooking up. "Dinner with No Name" is quite literally a thing in my house. Usually this blended banquet begins on one of those evenings where I'm tired (most evenings begin this way, honestly), I'm running low on food inventory because I didn't have time to run to the store that day (happens all too often), I maybe have a few containers of random leftovers I need to use up (Edward has heart palpitations at the thought of throwing food out), or I decide to get creative in the kitchen (a dolled-up way of saying "too lazy to open up a recipe book")—or all of the above!

As in everything in life, you win some and you lose some. On a rare occasion, I create a recipe that becomes a culinary triumph—but more often than not, it's a total and complete food fail. (FYI: Cereal and milk are a great dinner Plan B.) But I can proudly claim that one of our favorite comfort food all-in-ones, this Thanksgiving casserole, began as a nameless meal. I fancy thinking this dish is kind of like the amazing Willy Wonka's three-course-meal Thanksgiving Gum—but without the pie flavor or the round and bloated rolling purple kid at the end.

INGREDIENTS

- 2 boxes turkey stuffing
- Two 12 oz. cans evaporated milk
- 1 cup salted butter, melted
- 3-4 lbs. sliced turkey breasts
- 6 cups mashed potatoes (leftovers, premade, or instant)
- 12 oz. turkey gravy (leftover, premade, or instant)
- Note: If you're family isn't wild about turkey, use chicken breasts, chicken stuffing, and chicken gravy.

INSTRUCTIONS

1. Preheat oven to 425°F (218°C).
2. Prepare stuffing in a large bowl by adding the melted butter and substituting the evaporated milk in place of the water. Mix well with a fork.
3. Place turkey breasts in the bottom of a well-greased casserole dish.
4. Using a large spoon, spread the potatoes across the top of the turkey in an even layer.
5. Layer stuffing on top of potatoes.
6. Pour gravy on top.
7. Cover dish with tinfoil.
8. Place casserole on top of a shallow baking pan in case of spillover.
9. Bake in center of the oven for 45–60 minutes.

TIP

Once a week, dump the refrigerator! Take all the leftovers from previous meals, reheat them thoroughly, and serve a la carte for a Leftover Night dinner. It's a hodgepodge offering that is sure to have a dish to please everyone! And if you don't have enough leftovers to feed your whole crowd, throw out some bread and lunchmeat as an option too.

Homemade Potpourri

SUPPLIES

- 1 cup dried orange and apple slices
- 1 cup dried anise stars
- 1 cup dried rosehips
- 1 cup whole cloves
- 1 cup cinnamon sticks
- For an adorable addition, mix in a handful of Gingie Kids (Nonedible) Ornaments (see page 134)!

This is a great project to make as a gift for family and friends.

I believe one of the best ways to truly get in the spirit of the season is to give your home all the smelly smells of the holiday. I have a thing about scents—I may not trust my sense of direction, but I always trust my sense of smell. Like how I can sniff out a cup of spoiled milk faster than it takes me to untag that ugly side-profile photo my sister posted of me on Facebook.

There are certain aromas that trigger lovely memories of my childhood and my past. The tangy essence of bread-and-butter pickles at once puts my mind back to my grandparents' Christmassy dining room, where a smorgasbord of relish dishes, crackers, and snacks always completely covered the long table for grazing. A whiff of anise takes me to Edward's grandmother's small, homey kitchen full of family and piles of freshly baked pizzelles on the table and counters.

This homemade potpourri mingles all the fragrances of the holiday season to create a yummy mixed blend for snouts big and small. Not only is it pleasing to the nose, it's quite pretty to look at too!

INSTRUCTIONS

1. If you do not have a dehydrator, you can place thinly sliced fruit straight on your oven rack set at the lowest setting—250°F (120°C)—until dried out (about 2–3 hours), turning them every half hour or so. The fruit will stick to a tray, which is why they should be placed directly on the rack.
2. Mix all the ingredients together in a large bowl or container.
3. Set the dry potpourri out in a bowl or place it in a pot of boiling water to simmer over the stovetop.

This homemade potpourri mingles all the fragrances of the holiday season to create a yummy mixed blend for snouts big and small.

GREAT GIFTS TO SPREAD THE LOVE

There's something about my husband Edward that you should know: he's quite possibly the kindest person on the planet. Seriously. He's a friend to all, a master peacekeeper, and a helper to anyone who needs it. He's all the good you'd want in a neighbor, all the heart you'd want in your child's schoolteacher, and the very best half of our parenting duo. And because crucially important family values like compassion and empathy are caught, not taught, there is no better example of what I hope my children to be when they're grown than the big guy who's right beside me as I raise them up.

These craft and cooking ideas are an ideal way to teach your kids all about the merit of giving while spending precious time with them making a gift intended for others. From easy and quick presentations to crafts that require slightly more focus, you're sure to find something here to show a little thoughtfulness, love, and affection to any lucky recipient.

Rainbow Centerpiece
(page 34)

Lazy Susan Herb Planter
(page 72)

S'more S'mores
(page 82)

Mug Sweater
(page 128)

Homemade Potpourri
(page 118)

Hot Cocoa Snowman
(page 136)

Grinch Cookies
(page 140)

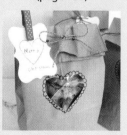

Cookie Bag
(page 142)

RAINY DAYS & DELIGHTFUL GOODIES

TASTY AND FUN ACTIVITIES FOR WHEN YOU'RE STUCK INSIDE

I'd be lying if I said I don't look forward to the occasional rain-all-day-long day. It gives me an excuse to stay inside and catch up on laundry, dirty dishes, or housekeeping (or even do none of those things and just lay around getting lost in a good book). I've also found rainy days to be some of the very best times to just be with the kids. A rainy day is a perfect excuse to do the little, unplanned things that wind up being the big things.

Don't get me wrong—we love to spend our days running around outside, swimming, going for walks, and taking bike rides, but sometimes the weather just won't cooperate, and you're forced to admit defeat and spend the day around the kitchen table. Well, your kids won't feel glum anymore when you whip out one of these crafts or recipes. They'll look forward to the next rainy day as much as I do when they realize they'll get to make more treats and projects like these.

Pet Silhouette
(page 20)

Dog Treats
(page 26)

Gingie Cookie Kids & Easiest Royal Icing Ever
(page 132)

Chocolate Chip Oatmeal Banana Bars
(page 46)

Homemade Applesauce
(page 92)

Gingie Kids (Nonedible) Ornaments
(page 134)

Sunflower Wreath
(page 76)

CHAPTER 4

Crushing the Winter Doldrums

No matter how old I get, the initial thrill of seeing those first snowflakes gracefully fall from the sky never seems to waver. Jumping up and down, clapping my hands, and squealing with delight is a guaranteed first-flake response from me. Each year, the kids and I all crowd around our picture window at the front of the house, watching the white stuff drop to the ground. It's incredible how such a small moment becomes a tradition without ever realizing the significance. I imagine the annual view, but instead of looking out, I think of what I would see looking in. Glimpses of the same people, but the faces and bodies growing and changing over time. Chubby babies cradled at my side turn into tall, lanky bodies front and center in the window. A pink-cheeked little girl with ponytails grows into a beautiful young woman in glasses. It's heartwarming and sad all at once. The crushing reality that no matter how hard I try to keep them small, the seasons change, and my little people change right along with them.

But all that fluffy and cold stuff brings along more than just higher furnace bills and heavy, drown-myself-in-a-tub-of-Ben-&-Jerry's feelings. They also usher in the beginning of a season packed full of all things joyfully merry and the opportunity to practice goodwill and giving. As a family, we've volunteered at the meal center, donated gently used toys that are no longer played with, filled bags with essential items for local shelters, and adopted families for Christmas. It's an opportunity for us to selflessly serve others—not only monetarily, but by gifting our time and talent to those in need. It's a chance to reflect on how fortunate we are to have a warm spot to place our heads at night and a family who's always nearby to love, argue, and arm wrestle with. More than anything, I believe that's what the season of goodwill is all about.

FRANK CAPRA'S
IT'S A WONDERFUL LIFE
ORIGINAL UNCUT VERSION

JAMES STEWART   DONNA REED

Merry Christmas

Winter
is a cold
time, but also
a time of warmth
and welcome.

welcome

Cozy Coaster

SUPPLIES

- Wide-mouth mason jar lids
- ¾" (2cm) pom-pom balls
- Felt
- Fabric scissors
- Black pencil
- Hot glue gun

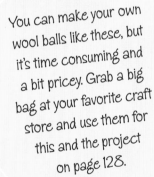

You can make your own wool balls like these, but it's time consuming and a bit pricey. Grab a big bag at your favorite craft store and use them for this and the project on page 128.

Do you have a favorite word? One that resonates with you or speaks to your soul? *Sleep, ice cream,* and *quiet* are definitely some of my favorite words. But one of my absolute favorite words would have to be *cozy*.

I adore ALL the cozy things. Blankets, sweaters, pillows, bear hugs—anything giving off those comfy vibes is the kind of thing I want to have around me. Snug as a little bug in a soft, fuzzy rug, so to speak. You know what else is soft and fuzzy and everything comfy? Pom-pom balls!

I like big pom-pom balls and I cannot lie. I've got a thing for those fuzzy, vibrant spheres. They are totally H.O.T. in the crafting world right now, and I'm not mad about it. The colors are plentiful, the price is downright cheap, and the creative possibilities are endless, which is why I'm giving you a 2-for-1 using these bad boys—two different projects so you can incorporate them however you want. You won't believe how these little balls can literally make something out of nothing with just a bit of trusty hot glue.

This coaster project is a perfect example. A few wide-mouth mason jar lids turn into adorable side table accompaniments and a perfect spot to plop your cuppa. They're an ideal cozy addition to an already cozy activity—drinking the calming tea or the warm, caffeinating coffee that we all crave. Turn to page 128 for the other super pom-pom project!

INSTRUCTIONS

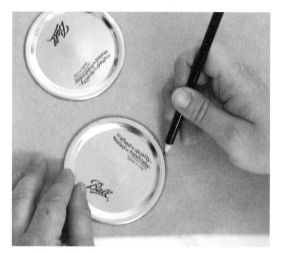

1 **Trace the lid.** Trace a mason jar lid multiple times (once for each coaster) onto your piece of felt using the black pencil. Cut each circle out with fabric scissors.

2 **Assemble the base.** Hot glue a felt circle to the underside of each lid.

3 **Check the fit.** Before beginning to glue, place pom-poms onto the lid to get an idea of the arrangement that will fill the lid the best. For my lids, it was an outer ring of balls, an inner ring of balls, and a ball in the center.

4 **Glue the pom-poms.** Taking one ball at a time, slowly hot glue the pom-poms onto the top of the lid until the space is full.

Cup Tray

Breaks from school mean my whole crew is at home. It's all ten of us squished inside our house, getting some serious QT—which makes this mama totally thrilled! I really do love it when my people are home together under one roof. It does my heart some good, way better than Honey Nut Cheerios ever could. It also means that my house is a mess all the time. Some days I swear my back is the only one that is capable of bending to pick something up off the floor, and I'm certainly the only one who seems to mind that you cannot find the kitchen countertop underneath all the toys, books, papers, and random dishes and cups that were left behind by their users.

To cut down on the kitchen clutter, I made this cup tray. It's just a plain wood tray with numbered circles (a circle for each member of the house). Once you get a cup out for the day, you place it on your circle and that is *your* cup *all* day. No more dishwashers full of a gazillion cups—just one cup per person, thank you very much!

Mug Sweater

SUPPLIES

- Your favorite travel mug
- Large piece of felt
- ¾" (2cm) pom-pom balls (in coordinating colors to felt)
- Black pencil
- Fabric scissors
- Hot glue gun
- Twine or yarn (optional)

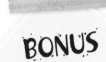

BONUS

This design also works as an adorable storage canister! Make one to hold your paintbrushes, your makeup supplies, or even facial tissues.

I know I'm not alone with my love for warm drinks and sweater weather. Just as the meals get heavier with all the comfort food I love to eat during this cooler time of year, unfortunately, so does my midsection. Any opportunity I can get to wear an oversized, hide-it-all cozy shirt with stretchy pants? I'll take it. Plus, the getup pairs so well with my daily messy bun and crooked glasses. Throw in a soft sofa, a fuzzy throw blanket, and a good book, and you've created my idea of comfy heaven.

I'll never forget the time Edward came home from work and, before he even put his bag down, looked me over and told me how good I looked. Not because he doesn't do that often (he does). And not because I had actually done something with myself (I hadn't). But because I was sporting a brand-spankin'-new, pill-free pair of butter yellow sweatpants! It was at this point that I realized maybe I had taken the "grungy Mom" look to a whole new level. Shortly after this, I upgraded my wardrobe to include a handful of slimming yoga pants to switch things up a bit—just for Edward!

I think most of us can agree that cold mornings are most definitely not the same without a pair of cozy sweatpants or a steaming cup of liquid caffeine. So why shouldn't our favorite travel mugs have a warm and comfy lil' getup too? Now you can take your fave winter drink and commuter cup on the go in style with a custom mug sweater. It is literally the perf sweater—stretchy, forgiving, and keeps your stuff warm. It's precisely the bit of extra your liquid caffeine never knew it needed!

TIP

If you spill some drink on your mug sweater or on your coaster (see page 124), simply wash under warm water with a dab of dish soap and allow to air dry.

1 **Trace the mug base.** Trace the bottom of your travel mug onto the felt using a black pencil.

2 **Cut the felt.** Next, measure and mark a 12" x 4" (30.5 x 10cm) strip of felt. Using fabric scissors, cut out the strip and the circle, allowing an additional ½" (1.5cm) around the circle. The cut doesn't have to be exact!

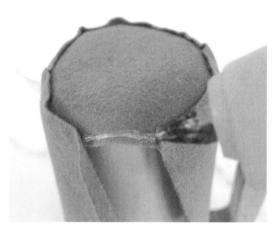

3 **Start gluing the casing.** Invert the mug onto your workspace. Place (but do not glue) the felt circle on the base of the upside-down mug with the traced lines facing up. With the hot glue gun, working in 1" (2.5cm) sections at a time, run a length of glue along the edge of the extra width of the circle and adhere part of the felt strip.

4 **Glue all the way around.** Work your way all around the circle to fully adhere the felt strip. You will notice the felt circle will begin to bunch while you are attaching to the strip. This is a good thing!

5 **Finish the casing assembly.** Once you get to the final section of felt, make sure you pull the end piece tight around the mug, and then glue the overlapping sections of felt to seal the assembly. You want a taut, snug fit on the mug to keep it in place when you're carrying it.

6 **Add pom-poms.** Hot glue pom-poms onto the felt casing, beginning at the bottom and working in rows, making sure the balls are pressed tightly together.

7 **Work your way up.** Continue gluing and moving up with the pom-pom rows until the felt is fully covered.

8 **Add a bow.** Add a bow with twine (yarn would be cute too!). This step is optional, but I like to do everything a little extra. It's just how I roll.

Gingie Cookie Kids & Easiest Royal Icing Ever

INGREDIENTS

- 3 cups flour
- 1½ tsp. baking powder
- ¾ tsp. baking soda
- ¼ tsp. salt
- 1 tbsp. ground ginger
- 1¾ tsp. ground cinnamon
- ¼ tsp. ground cloves
- 6 tbsp. unsalted butter
- ¾ cup brown sugar
- 1 large egg
- ½ cup molasses
- 2 tsp. vanilla extract

For the icing:

- 1 cup powdered sugar
- ½ tsp. vanilla extract
- 2 tbsp. water or milk (I prefer milk)
- Gel food coloring (optional)

One of my most favorite appliances in my kitchen is my vintage avocado-colored oven. It is big, green, and tough—so it's only fitting that we've named him "The Hulk." As a woman who spends a substantial amount of time in her kitchen, trying to keep all those small and big mouths fed and watered on the daily, I truly appreciate the convenience of having a double oven. It was a sad day indeed when the range that came with our home took its last dying breath while baking up a couple frozen pizzas. But it was all totally worth not having an oven for a week and surviving on oatmeal and popcorn until we were able to bring this retro machine home. The green monstrosity just fits our kitchen like it was meant to be there, and it works like Betty Crocker's dream. I often think of all the casseroles, roasts, and desserts through the past fifty years that were lovingly created using the big guy. Can you imagine the dishes? All the fad casseroles and breaded SPAM platters this thing has seen?

Even though I've used this incredible oven daily for more than three years, if there's one thing the jolly green giant has baked an enormous amount of since he's been in this house, it's cookies. Not to toot my own Pastry Chef horn, but I'm kind of known to bake a fantastic cookie. These gingie cookie kids are not an exception. With just the slightest hint of molasses, they have a traditional gingerbread flavor that's great for gingerbread boy and girl cutters. Plus, they are simply divine with a cup of coffee on a cold winter's morning!

Let the kids do the decorating—they will be so pleased to get creative and make each yummy cookie look different!

INSTRUCTIONS

1. Preheat oven to 375°F (190°C). Prepare baking sheets by spraying with nonstick spray or lining with parchment paper.
2. In a large bowl, combine the dry ingredients: dry flour, baking powder, baking soda, salt, ginger, cinnamon, and cloves. Note: Correct measurements make or break this recipe. Too much flour will make it dry, and too little will make it too sticky. The best way to avoid this is to measure the flour into a small bowl, sift, and then measure it a second time (chances are high there will be extra flour left over that you will not add back).
3. Using your stand mixer or a hand mixer, beat butter, brown sugar, and egg until well blended.
4. Pour in molasses and vanilla.
5. Gradually add dry ingredients and mix until thoroughly mixed.
6. With a floured countertop, roll out small portions of dough at a time and cut with cookie cutters, or simply add to a greased 9" x 13" (23 x 33cm) sheet pan for a slab cookie.
7. Space cookies approximately 1½" (4cm) apart. Bake one sheet at a time for 7–10 minutes. Less time will give you softer, chewier cookies; more time will give you more of a crunch. Both are delicious!
8. Let cool, then decorate with icing. To make icing, mix all ingredients together. A stand mixer works best if you've got one. You may need to add more powdered sugar if it's not thick enough, or more milk if it's too thick. Add food coloring if desired.

Gingie Kids (Nonedible) Ornaments

SUPPLIES

- 1 cup cinnamon
- 1 tbsp. ground cloves
- 1 tbsp. ground nutmeg
- ¾ cup applesauce
- 2 tbsp. white craft glue
- Gingerbread man cookie cutter (or cookie cutters in any desired shapes)

If you enjoyed making the edible Gingie Cookie Kids on the previous page, but they all got eaten up too fast, you can make these nonedible decorative Gingie Kid versions! They're made with craft glue, so although they're nontoxic, they're definitely NOT to snack on! But they'll make your home smell just as delectably amazing. Not to mention, they're just the cutest lil' ornament guys and look so adorable hanging on your family Christmas tree. You could even string 'em up in a row and make a decorative garland! And, as always, they're so simple to make using ingredients you probably already have in your pantry.

The kids and I made these one year after our dog ate ALL of our gingerbread cookies while we were out looking at Christmas lights. He figured out how to climb the table (we still don't understand how he did it) and ate every single leftover cookie. Luckily (for him and for us), we had already eaten a bunch ourselves, but he must have really felt that he was missing out on the sweet fun. After we got all of our giggles out (and the poor boy's tummy settled down), we decided to make some ornaments to remember this funny Christmas story!

Bonus: If you have a house-shaped cookie cutter, make sure to cut out a few adorable Gingie Homes to go along with your Gingie Kids!

These ornaments will make your home smell just as delectably amazing as the edible cookie on page 132!

INSTRUCTIONS

1. Preheat oven to 200°F (93°C). You can also omit the oven and let the ornaments air dry in a sunny spot for four or five days.

2. Stir together the cinnamon, cloves, and nutmeg. Mix in the applesauce and glue. Whip the mixture with a stand mixer or just your hands for a few minutes until a ball forms. If the mix is too gooey, add more cinnamon. If it's too dry, add more applesauce.

3. Lightly dust your work surface with cinnamon. Roll out the dough to approximately ¼" (0.5cm) thick. Using your desired cookie cutter shapes, cut out the shapes and place them on a nonstick sprayed pan. Don't forget to punch a hole at the top using a toothpick or skewer if you wish to hang the ornaments with ribbon or add a bow.

4. Bake for 3 hours and allow to cool completely. Your ornaments are ready for hanging! (And NOT for eating.)

Hot Cocoa Snowman

SUPPLIES

- 3 glass bowls, one 18" (46cm) round and two 15" (38cm) round, that stack on top of one another (find them at craft or dollar stores)
- Adhesive dots
- 2–3 black buttons
- 2" x 18" (5 x 46cm) length of wide ribbon
- Doll top hat
- Dry hot cocoa mix
- Unwrapped peppermint candies
- Mini marshmallows

TIP

The supplies and instructions call for attaching classic black buttons to your snowman, but you can also use red felt cutout hearts as I have done here!

Listen, I'll be the first to admit: we have a lot of rules at our house. I feel it's the only way to keep things steady and balanced. While my husband truly believes rules are made to be broken (FYI: It would have been great if someone could have filled me in on the whole "having a husband is actually similar to raising a child" thing beforehand. Alas.), I believe some rules are absolute and unbreakable. Our Hot Cocoa rule is one such mandate. *If we go sledding, we drink hot cocoa.* Seriously. In a very "let it be written, let it be done" manner, we do not break hot cocoa protocol. I don't even know what the penalty would be, but I'm confident it would Not. Be. Good.

And let's be clear, we're not talking about just any old mug of chocolatey drink. I'm referring to a piping hot, foamy milk chocolate cocoa with marshmallows, cinnamon, whipped cream, Pirouette wafer sticks, and candy canes for the top. If I'm feeling extra lovey, I'll throw in some sprinkles too. There's no denying that there's just something about hot cocoa that warms you from the top of your head to the tip of your toes after you've been tramping around in all that fluffy and cold white stuff for a few hours.

In this house, we love our cocoa so much that I create a Hot Cocoa Bar in our kitchen for the entire snowy season that has all the necessary fixings readily available for our home full of hot chocolate aficionados. It's literally a "just add drink" setup. This hot cocoa snowman is the quintessential addition to our cocoa station. We keep mugs on mug hooks in a row on the wall behind the snowman to allow for easy access and to complete the look of the cocoa bar. The snowman also makes a great gift for a neighbor!

INSTRUCTIONS

1 **Fill the bowls.** Fill the bowls, one ingredient per bowl. Fill the largest bowl with hot cocoa mix and the two smaller bowls with peppermints and marshmallows.

2 **Stack the bowls.** Carefully stack the bowls with the cocoa on the bottom, the marshmallows in the middle, and the peppermints on top. For additional security, if desired, apply adhesive dots along the top rims of the bowls to keep them steady while they sit on the top of each other. This is an especially good idea if you plan to move the snowman often. (The dots won't create a permanent bond.)

3 **Add the top hat.** Using adhesive dots, attach the top hat to the rim of the top bowl.

4 **Add the buttons.** Adhere the buttons to the fronts of the middle and bottom bowls using adhesive dots.

5 **Add the ribbon.** For the scarf, wrap the ribbon loosely between the top and middle bowls, crossing one end over the other and using an adhesive dot to hold it in place.

Seek-and-Find Activity Balls

Whip up this activity in just ten minutes to keep the kids occupied during long car rides.

If you're going over the river and through the woods to visit a dear loved one, keep the littles busy with this fun and festive activity. Hey—I get it! It's a busy season, and sometimes adding one more thing to the list that never ends just seems like too much. But this takes less than ten minutes to make from start to finish—totally doable and totally worth it if it cuts down on at least three "Are we there yets," right?

To make each seek-and-find activity ball, take a clear plastic ball ornament, drop in a selection of baubles, beads, figurines, and other miscellaneous miniature trinkets, and then fill the rest of the ornament almost full with white foam balls (the kind you can buy at the craft store). Hot glue the top of the ornament closed to prevent accidental spilling. You can choose to make the hidden items random or themed.

To do the activity, either make a list of what you put into each ornament beforehand and have the kids search for each item on the list, or just put a certain number of items into each ornament for them to find without a guiding list. The kids can pass the balls around to defeat each one, and even time themselves to see who can find all the items the fastest! It should keep them occupied for at least part of any long car ride.

Grinch Cookies

INGREDIENTS

- 1¼ cups flour
- ¼ tsp. baking soda
- ¼ tsp. salt
- ½ cup salted butter
- ¼ cup sugar
- ¾ cup brown sugar
- 1 large egg
- 1 tsp. vanilla
- Green food coloring
- Red or pink heart sprinkles

For the cinnamon sugar mix:
- ¼ cup green colored sugar
- 2 tbsp. cinnamon

I can't help but think if the famously grumpy and fuzzy Christmas-detesting and socially prickly guy was a baked dessert, it would look just like these Grinch cookies that my family makes every holiday season for our cookie platters. A little ugly and very green with a heart that's no longer two sizes too small! We typically make a movie night out of it, watching the big green grumpy guy on screen while making and baking (and, of course, eating) these fun treats. I always make sure to have plenty of red sprinkle hearts on hand in our baking center. I never know when my oldest girl will get the itch to make a few batches of her favorite cookies throughout the holiday season, and, obviously, no one complains when she does! No matter if you're serving from a plate stacked high with them or from a platter showcasing a variety of cookie flavors, everyone recognizes these classic Grinch Cookies.

It's fine if your kids want to add more than a single heart sprinkle to each cookie—the more love, the better!

INSTRUCTIONS

1. Preheat oven to 350°F (175°C).
2. Sift the flour, baking soda, and salt together. Set aside.
3. In another bowl, cream the butter with sugar and brown sugar.
4. Mix in egg and vanilla.
5. Add the dry mixture to the wet mixture and add ten drops of food coloring, mixing well until blended.
6. Refrigerate dough for an hour.
7. Make the cinnamon sugar mix by combining ingredients in a bowl.
8. Form dough into 1" (2.5cm) balls and roll the ball into sugar mix.
9. Bake 10–12 minutes.
10. Place a heart sprinkle on each cookie while they're still warm. Cool on wire rack.

This is a truly festive treat that's perfect to have on hand to take to friends' homes over the holidays.

Cookie Bag

SUPPLIES

- Paper lunch bags
- Scrap cardboard
- Hobby/craft knife
- Pencil
- Hole punch
- Clear cellophane
- Clear tape
- Black marker
- Ribbon
- Plain gift tags
- Stamp and ink
- Clothespin (optional)

We've all heard the saying "sharing is caring." What you probably didn't realize is that this iconic phrase is most especially true when it comes to people and cookies. Giving a bag or box of warm, freshly baked chocolate chip cookies is something we really enjoy doing for our neighbors and friends on snow days when the kids have been called off school and the day is whatever we want to make it. Delivering these treats is a way of checking in with the people around us during inclement weather while sharing some ooey gooey, sweet and yummy goodness. Edward typically rounds up the older kids and they shovel the driveways around us while I stay inside with the younger kids and bake up lots of trays of chocolatey love.

And not much says "I love you" or "You're a great neighbor" or "Sorry my dog is a barking nutcase" quite like a bag full of delicious cookies and a handwritten note. The youngsters (with a little help from you) can create this darling cookie bag to deliver all the warm and fuzzy feelings, as well as those yummy goodies, in just a few minutes! This project is just about as kid-friendly as you can get.

Fill these gift bags with the baked goodies on pages 140, 148, or 154!

Merr y
Christmas

Not much says "I love you" or
"You're a great neighbor" or "Sorry
my dog is a barking nutcase" quite
like a bag full of delicious cookies
and a handwritten note.

INSTRUCTIONS

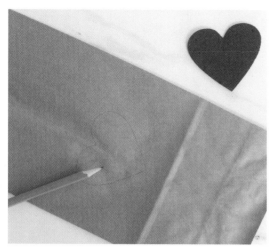

1 **Draw the heart.** Trace or freehand draw a 3" (8cm) heart onto the front of the bag.

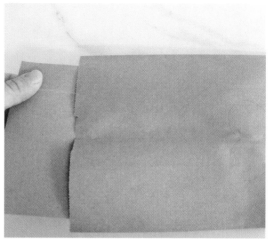

2 **Insert cardboard.** Insert a piece of scrap cardboard into the folded bag to lie underneath the drawn heart shape.

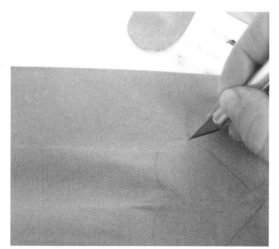

3 **Cut out the heart.** Using a hobby/craft knife, cut out the heart from the front of the bag.

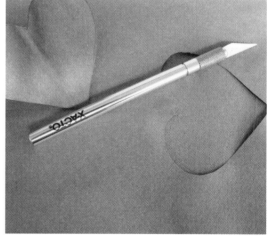

4 **Take out the cardboard.** Remove the cardboard from the inside of the bag and the heart from the outside to reveal your heart-shaped hole.

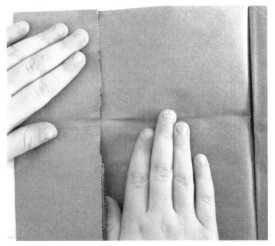

5 **Fold the bag.** Fold over the top of the bag about 2" (5cm).

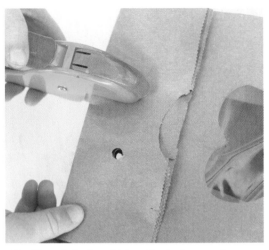

6 **Punch holes.** Using the hole punch, make two holes in the center of the folded opening about 1" (2.5cm) apart. Punch all the way through all layers.

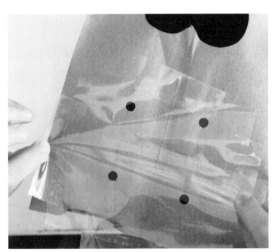

7 **Prepare cellophane.** Cut a 3" x 3" (8 x 8cm) square of cellophane and add a piece of tape to all four edges.

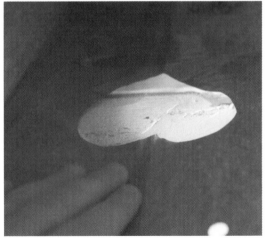

8 **Attach the cellophane.** Unfold the top of the bag. Attach the taped cellophane to the interior front of the bag, making sure the plastic covers the heart completely, but not the punched holes.

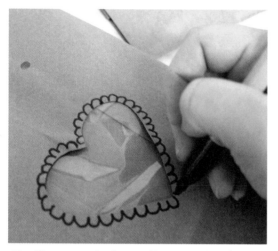

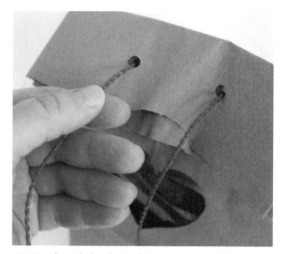

9 **Decorate the heart.** For an optional decorative touch, add a scalloped trim along the outside edge of the heart with black marker.

10 **Load the bag.** Fill your bag with cookies. Fold the top down again and run a 16" (41cm) length of ribbon through the holes, making sure the ribbon ends are sticking out at the front of the bag.

11 **Make the tag.** Customize a gift tag by stamping a heart onto the tag and having the kids write "Merry Christmas" or "Made with Love" on it.

12 **Add the tag.** Thread the tag onto the ribbon before tying the ribbon into a bow, or clip the tag to the top of the bag with a clothespin.

Gift Wrap Matters

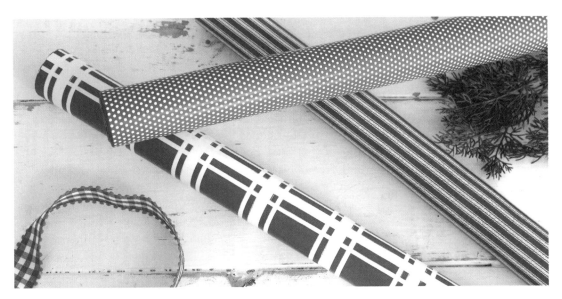

I've tried it all, folks, from wrapping gifts weeks or even months in advance, to waiting until after midnight Mass on Christmas Eve. (By the way, I rate the latter 0 out of 0, would NOT recommend. "Procrastinate now and panic later" is definitely not the MO you should adopt on December 24th.) Wrapping presents in the days leading up to the Jolly Big Man's visit can be a time-consuming and stressful chore for parents. The kids are in the house, the calendar is full of engagements, and you have an endless list of last-minute errands to handle. I swear I lose a quarter of my hair in December due to the anxiety of making it the "perfect" Christmas for my family.

Here's the thing—not one single year is ever perfect to my standards. It seems to always wind up more of a messy sled-wreck than anything. My kids have been gifted gifts that, unbeknownst to us, were completely broken in the box. Once there was a Christmas gerbil that turned out to be the spawn of a gremlin and bit through my #2's finger, drawing blood and causing complete chaotic panic. Oh, and we cannot forget the year of the Christmas Flu—lots of bodily fluid cleanup that year (good times). But no matter what it looks like to Edward and me, in the kid's eyes, it's always perfectly magical. They see things so much differently than we adults do, with our tired and apprehensive views.

Something I've always done to decrease a bit of the hassle is to use a different gift wrap for each kid. Whether it's determined by color or by pattern, it's a surefire way to make you feel a little more organized—even if you are repeatedly losing the gift wrap tape, scissors, and name tags!

Best Ever Sugar Cookies

INGREDIENTS

- 1 cup salted butter, room temperature
- 3 large eggs
- 1 cup sour cream, room temperature
- 1 tsp. vanilla
- 2 cups sugar
- 1 tsp. baking soda
- 1 tsp. salt
- 2 tsp. baking powder
- 5 cups flour

TIP

I suggest not doubling this recipe—it is thick and may be too hard on your mixers. Instead, make separate batches. The dough can be prepared in advance and frozen.

Fun fact: I used to own my own Cottage Food Business (a home-based bakery). But I like to say "Cottage Bakery" because it sounds so much more trendy-chic. And I like to sound fancy any chance I can get. Anyway, I had four children at the time, and the business venture was a way for me to contribute to our household finances while staying home with my little people. Christmas was by far the busiest time of year for my company. I'd spend endless days baking and decorating and entire afternoons delivering trays upon trays of cookie platters all over northeastern Ohio. I learned a lot in those years about time management, marketing, people operations, and charging your worth. Unbeknownst to me, it was essentially life training for my future Boss Mom position of running a ten-person household for free. It also happens to be when I realized I should never underestimate the power of a promised McD's Happy Meal to keep the kids in line when they're bored out of their gourds in the van.

To this day, whenever I bake some of our favorite cookie recipes, I can't help but appreciate those years of standing in my kitchen mixing up ingredients, rolling out dough, and cutting out shapes. I was blessed to be able to do what I love, while being in the place I love, with the people I love. That's why my Christmas sugar cookies hold a special spot in my heart. They are literally a cookie par-tay in your mouth and the ultimate balance of soft and chewy. They're just supreme for classic cutout Christmas cookie shapes or bars.

INSTRUCTIONS

1. Preheat oven to 350°F (175°C). Line pan with parchment or baking mat.
2. Using a stand mixer or hand mixer, mix wet ingredients.
3. In a separate bowl, sift and mix dry ingredients.
4. Slowly add dry mixture to wet mixture using the mixer.
5. Chill dough thoroughly.
6. To make bar cookies, evenly press dough on greased and floured sheet pan. To make cutout cookies, flour counter, and, using small portions of dough at a time, roll out to ¼" (0.5cm) thickness, then cut out shapes.
7. Bake 10–13 minutes. Cookies will not look brown. If preparing bars in a large pan, baking time may require a few more minutes, depending on thickness of dough.
8. Allow to cool completely on cooling racks before frosting. Homemade cookie frosting is good, but typically, after a day of mixing, rolling, and cutting, this mama is tired, and a can of good ol' store-bought frosting does the trick just fine!

Feather Tree

SUPPLIES

- 17" (43cm) tree cone
- 75–100 pink or white feathers
- Hot glue gun
- Chunky pink or white yarn
- Fabric scissors
- 8" x 10" (20 x 25cm) piece of pink or white felt
- Velvet ribbon

Sometimes having a large family means finding the big things in the small moments. Take Valentine's Day, for example. It's most definitely still the day of big love for us, just no fancy restaurants or expensive gifts required. Edward and I celebrate the evening at home with the kids. They start their morning with little heart mailboxes stuffed with mini candies and a love letter from me. It's also the one night a year that they can expect to have a homemade surf 'n' turf meal, complete with a big bottle of their favorite steak sauce on the side. Yep—we get pretty swank around here. I even break out our good silver (passed down from my Auntie) and our china (secondhand but adorable), and I light some tapered candles on our fancy picnic-table-that's-actually-a-dining-room-table. We end it all with a big dessert that no one ever has room for, but that we all manage to eat after unbuttoning our pants.

The future mother-in-law (monster-in-law, possibly? Still to be determined...) in me can't help but hope that I'm teaching my small people that the whole of someone's love isn't based on the amount of money they spend, but by the accumulation of their actions and intentions—that "special" nights are made by the memories shared, no matter where you are. As long as you're with people who love you for exactly who you are, you are exactly where you should be. Isn't that what Valentine's Day, heck, any day when you're raising kids, is all about?

But that's not to say that you can't go nuts decorating your house for the day of perpetual hugs and kisses. I mean, it's the one opportunity I have all year to fill my house with a ridiculous amount of pink and purple hearts, loads of fake roses, a bunch of adorable almost-nakey cupids with tiny arrows, and some delightful feather trees—you better believe I'm not going to miss it! XOXOXO forever!

Little heart mailboxes stuffed with love letters.

I try to teach my small people that the whole of someone's love isn't based on the amount of money they spend, but by the accumulation of their actions and intentions.

1 **Start gluing feathers.**
Starting about 2" (5cm) from the bottom of the tree cone, hot glue the tip of a feather shaft to the tree, upside-down. Make sure the feather veins are curving out, not in. Continue gluing the feathers around the cone, one at a time, until you have made a complete row (see next step's photo).

2 **Finish all the feather rows.** Move up another 2" (5cm) and start a new row of feathers. Once you've worked your way to the top of the cone, the final row should be glued to the tip of the cone. Fill in any open spots on the tree with feathers. You don't want to see the tree cone at all through the feathers.

3 **Make a topper.** Make a topper using a chunky yarn tied in a bow. Tie it directly to the top of the tree and secure it with a dab of hot glue. You could also use traditional-sized yarn and wrap it around the tip with a bow.

4 **Cut the circle.** Trace a circle approximately 7" (18cm) wide onto a piece of 8" x 10" (20 x 25cm) felt using a bowl or plate in the right size. Cut out the circle using fabric scissors.

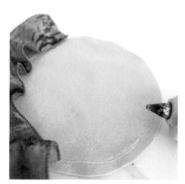

5 **Add the ribbon.** Working about 4" (10cm) at a time, hot glue the velvet ribbon to the felt circle, starting along the outside rim. Make sure to gather your ribbon as you glue, every few inches, to create a ruffled edge.

6 **Attach the base.** Gather and attach a second layer of ruffled ribbon just inside the first row. Then hot glue the base of the tree cone to the open circle in the middle of the ribbon.

Silver Storage

I was gifted a beautiful silver flatware set from my Auntie Annie. They were passed down to her by her mother, and I feel a sense of great honor to have them in my home. Instead of the gorgeous set being stored away in a box or drawer where no one can see them, I leave them out all year as a showpiece in my kitchen. We use the set during super special dinners, and, when they're not in use, I store the precious silverware in a cute glass jar with a rubber-sealed lid. I use a piece of non-slip grip shelf liner placed inside at the bottom of the jar as a soft cushion for the silverware to perch on. Simply cut a circle from the liner using the bottom of the jar as a template. And, to cut down on the moisture—which in turn cuts down on the tarnishing of the silver—I throw in a few silica gel packets (those little baggies you find in new shoe boxes or in the bottom of a new purse)!

Celebration Chocolate Chip Cookies

INGREDIENTS

- 1 cup salted butter, softened
- 1 cup vegetable shortening
- 1½ cups sugar
- 1½ cups brown sugar
- 2 tsp. vanilla
- 4 large eggs
- 5½ cups flour
- 2 tsp. baking soda
- 2 bags milk chocolate chips

The reason I named these bad boys "Celebration Chocolate Chip Cookies" is because they are ideal for any celebration, gala, or festivity, big or small. Birthdays, back to school, snow days, holidays, trips to the dentist, a successful day of cleaning your house ... whatever the reason, these cookies are the best way to salute the situation. And I know we've all seen loads of recipes that claim to be "The Best Chocolate Chip Cookies Ever," but those guys need to just sit down right this minute, because these chocolate chip cookies? They're *actually* the best in the world. Take the review straight from the mouth of my seven-year-old food critic and believe it, my friends.

INSTRUCTIONS

1. Preheat oven to 350°F (175°C).
2. Cream butter, shortening, sugar, brown sugar, and vanilla.
3. Stir in eggs.
4. Slowly add flour and baking soda to avoid splash-over. Beat until thoroughly mixed.
5. Fold in chocolate chips.
6. Drop by rolled teaspoonfuls onto baking sheet covered in parchment paper.
7. Bake 10–12 minutes.

Whatever the reason, these cookies are the best way to salute the situation.

TIP

This recipe works well for cookie bars. Simply follow the directions and spread the cookie dough into a greased sheet pan. Press the dough until evenly spread. Then bake at 350°F (175°C) for about 20 minutes.

Templates

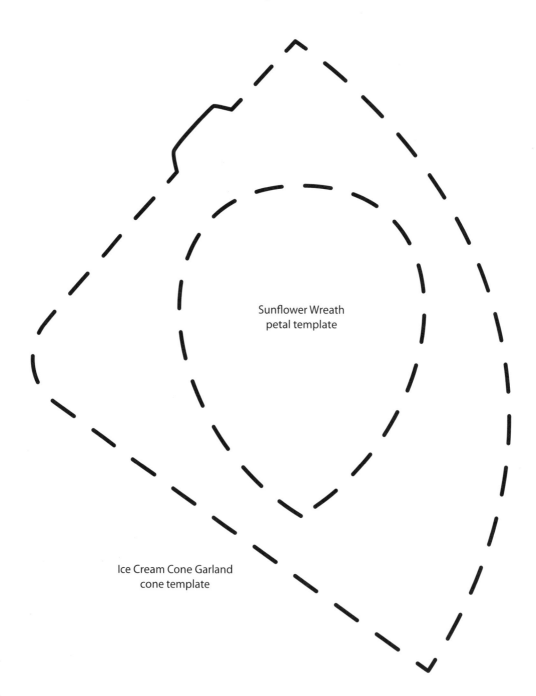

Sunflower Wreath
petal template

Ice Cream Cone Garland
cone template

School lunch
checklist

Protein :

Dairy :

Fruit :

Vegetable :

Grain :

Fun Treat :

Drink :

Lunch Checklist—photocopy and fill in!

About the Author

Kristin Gambaccini is a mom of many, a maker, and a baker.

She resides in Medina, a small town in Ohio, with her husband Edward, their eight children, two dogs, and three city chickens. When she's not driving her crew around town to their various sports and activities in their fifteen-passenger family van dubbed "The Gam-Bus," changing out laundry loads, or scrubbing toilets, you'll most likely find her hiding in a corner reading or out in her workshop jamming to '80s classics while making some sort of crafty crap.

Kristin is the author of the popular blog and social media pages Kristin Gambaccini Blog (formerly Perfectly DeStressed) (www.kristingambacciniblog.com), where she pens funny real-life mom stories, crafty home-betterment instructionals, entertaining hands-on busy activities for kids, and homemade(ish) recipes to feed a crowd. She's often seen—and heard—sharing her ideas and projects on local and national television as well as radio.

One thing is certain: whether you are an experienced crafter or a wannabe Pinterest Mom, you'll find a kindred spirit and a welcoming place with Kristin. She is a "door's always open" kind of friend—just be prepared to help fold a load of laundry or two while you're there.

Acknowledgments

I couldn't have done this without you, Edward. No matter where I am, I know you're right behind me—holding me up, watching me mess up, and pulling out all my stripped screws from the wall. Plus, you let me sleep in. I love you.

To my little (and not so little) children, you said it best when you said, "You get to write a book because of us." Very true. I also drink cheap wine often because of you. I love each one of you for exactly who you are on the inside to the moon and back a gazillion, bazillion times over again. You are my whole world.

To my parents, who just happen to be the best Mimi and Papa—Thank you for loving my children as much as you do and always ensuring the pool is clean, their candy supply is topped off, the donuts are open, and the ice cream is readily available, no matter where we are.

To Ed's parents, who just happen to be the best Grandma and Grandpa—Thank you for always putting all of us kids first and setting the example of what love in a home looks like. (And for always making our favorite foods.)

Brandi—I'm sorry. You're stuck with me. Forever. I couldn't love you or appreciate you more if I tried. I'm so darn proud to call you my best friend ever forever.

Auntie Annie—You get me. I get you.

To Amelia—Thank you for believing in me and giving this Medina homegirl a chance.

Fox Chapel—Thank you for this incredible opportunity!

Praise for This Book

"It takes someone special to turn a house into a home. Kristin's *Crafty Family Ideas* has a special blend of practical and fun that turns a house into something magical."

—Matt Fox, co-host of HGTV's first program, *Room by Room*

"As a busy working mom, I have a huge desire to craft with my kids but very little time to come up with the idea and prep for it. *Crafty Family Ideas* is the answer I've been looking for! Kristin takes the headache out of the planning. The projects are perfect for creating happy memories."

—Brittany Jepsen, author of *Craft the Rainbow*

"This is the kind of book I wish I had when I was a kid. A treasure chest of fun, very doable craft ideas and recipes. Now let's make, make, make . . ."

—Paul Lowe, founder of *Sweet Paul Magazine*

"There is a year's worth of play in this book that will keep the entire family entertained (not just the kids)! The ideas are so creative, colorful, and fun, yet doable. I am off to make a book pouch right now . . ."

—Holly Homer, founder of KidsActivities.com and best-selling author of *The Big Book of Kids Activities*

"Kristin is chock full of fun and easy ideas for rainy days, summer days, and holidays. Combine that with her delightful family stories and you've got a great resource for keeping your crew happy, creative, and well-fed!"

—Tabitha "Jo" Dotson, author of *Chica and Jo Craft with Nail Polish: 20+ Easy Projects for DIY Style*

"Filled with simple, fun craft projects to do with your kids in every season of the year, this book is a must-have for busy moms! It's also loaded with family-friendly recipes and tons of helpful tips from Kristin's experiences as a mom of eight."

—Amy Latta, television craft expert and author of *Hand Lettering for Relaxation*

"These accessible projects will provide hours of creative, non-screentime fun."

—Ramona Cruz-Peters, mother, cookbook author, and Editor-in-Chief of FabEveryday.com

"Great for any family that needs a little guidance when it comes to 'doing things.' Everyday life can become mundane, and this book is the perfect all-around guide with cooking ideas, crafts, and activities to add that little 'extra' to everyday family life. You can go from front cover to back cover and have enough variety that you won't get bored. It's not all craft and it's not all cooking—it's a perfect blend of typical family life."

—Shellie Wilson, CraftGossip.com Chief Editor and COO

"Kristin Gambaccini has compiled a varied and ambitious family crafts book at exactly the right time, when we're all trying to keep our children and ourselves busy and reclaim some time away from the screens."

—Robert Haynes-Peterson, lifestyle writer, Happify.com

"Looking for fun and colorful ideas to celebrate the season or brighten up a rainy day with a craft? This creative guide is filled with unique DIY projects that are easy and inexpensive, and the step-by-step instructions make them easy for everyone."

—Amy Bizzarri, Chicago-based author and teacher and contributor to WeAreTeachers.com

"Kristin has curated a terrific range of craft projects that you can do by yourself or with your family. The beauty of this book is Kristin's experience as a mother of eight; there are tons of tips on working with your kids, organizing your household, and much more. You'll enjoy the projects, but you'll keep coming back for the wisdom!"

—Jamie "MrXStitch" Chalmers, founder of *XStitch Magazine*

"This book teaches kids to be creative, a skill that, if nurtured, will serve them well their whole lives long!"

—Nancy Monson, author of *Craft to Heal: Soothing Your Soul with Sewing, Painting, and Other Pastimes*

Index

Note: Page numbers in parentheses indicate templates.

activity balls, seek-and-find, 139
apples
  Candy Apples (Nonedible), 88–90
  Homemade Applesauce, 92–93
  Perfectly Perfect Apple Pie, 108–9
art and home decor
  Art Display, 31
  Candy Apples (Nonedible), 88–90
  Cozy Coaster, 124–26
  Cup Tray, 127
  Drinking Glass Flower Vase, 37
  Feather Tree, 150–52
  Gingie Kids (Nonedible) Ornaments, 134–35
  Homemade Potpourri, 118–19
  Hot Cocoa Snowman, 136–38
  Ice Cream Cone Garland, 60–64 (156)
  Lazy Susan Herb Planter, 72–74
  Pet Silhouette, 20–24
  Pumpkin Pie Garland, 110–14
  Rainbow Centerpiece, 34–36
  Silver Storage, 153
  Sunflower Wreath, 76–80 (156)
  Tin Can Art Storage, 28–30

bedtime routine, 17
birthday parties, ideas for, 85
Birthday Party Craft, 65
Book Pouch, 68–71
Bubblegum Machine, 52–56
bug spray, homemade, 75
buttons, candy corn, 100–104

Candy Corn Buttons, 100–104
Caramel Corn Snack, 58–59
Carrot Cake, 38–39
chalk, sidewalk popsicle, 40–44
chocolate
  about: S'mores Station, 81
  Celebration Chocolate Chip Cookies, 154–55
  Chocolate Chip Oatmeal Banana Bars, 46–47
  Homemade(ish) Dr. Cake, 66–67
  No-Bake Energy Balls, 32–33
  S'mores S'mores, 82–83
coaster, cozy, 124–26
Cookie Bag, 142–46
cookies. See recipes (winter)

crafting, family and
  about: this book and, 6–7
  author's family and, 8–11
  birthday parties, special treats, 85
  favorites for single kids, 84
  gift ideas, 120
  group activities and feeding a crowd, 48
  organizational ideas, 49
  rainy-day ideas, 121
Cup Tray, 127

desserts. See recipes
Dog Treats, 26–27

Eggshell Planting, 25
energy balls, no-bake, 32–33

Feather Tree, 150–52

Game Day, 115
garlands, 60–64 (156), 110–14
gift ideas, 120
gift wrap tips, 147
Gingie Cookie Kids & Easiest Royal Icing Ever, 132–33
Gingie Kids (Nonedible) Ornaments, 134–35
Grinch Cookies, 140–41

herb planter, 72–74
home decor. See art and home decor

Ice Cream Cone Garland, 60–64 (156)

lunches, packed, 91 (157)

Mug Sweater, 128–31

organizational ideas, 49
ornaments, 134–35, 139

pets
  Dog Treats, 26–27
  Pet Silhouette, 20–24
pie. See recipes (fall)
plants
  Eggshell Planting, 25
  Lazy Susan Herb Planter, 72–74
Popsicle Stick Numbers, 45
potpourri, homemade, 118–19
projects and bright ideas (fall), 86–119
  about: life on the porch, 86; storage canister, 128

Candy Apples (Nonedible), 88–90
Candy Corn Buttons, 100–104
Game Day, 115
Homemade Potpourri, 118–19
Jack-o'-Lantern Candy Holder, 94–96
Packed Lunches, 91 (157)
Pumpkin Pie Garland, 110–14
Pumpkin Saver, 97
projects and bright ideas (spring), 12–47. See also recipes (spring)
  about: spring break fun, 12
  Art Display, 31
  Drinking Glass Flower Vase, 37
  Eggshell Planting, 25
  Embellished Umbrella, 14–16
  Mommy Daddy Nights, 17
  Pet Silhouette, 20–24
  Rainbow Centerpiece, 34–36
  Sidewalk Popsicle Chalk, 40–44
  Tin Can Art Storage, 28–30
projects and bright ideas (summer), 50–83. See also recipes (summer)
  about: creative summer, 50
  Birthday Party Craft, 65
  Book Pouch, 68–71
  Bubblegum Machine, 52–56
  Homemade Bug Spray, 75
  Ice Cream Cone Garland, 60–64 (156)
  Lazy Susan Herb Planter, 72–74
  Sunflower Wreath, 76–80 (156)
  Vacation Travel, 57
projects and bright ideas (winter), 122–55
  about: crushing winter doldrums, 122; gift wrap tips, 147
  Cookie Bag, 142–46
  Cozy Coaster, 124–26
  Cup Tray, 127
  Feather Tree, 150–52
  Gingie Kids (Nonedible) Ornaments, 134–35
  Hot Cocoa Snowman, 136–38
  Mug Sweater, 128–31
  Seek-and-Find Activity Balls, 139
  Silver Storage, 153

pumpkins
  Dinner in a Pumpkin, 98–99
  Jack-o'-Lantern Candy Holder, 94–96
  Pumpkin Pie Garland, 110–14
  Pumpkin Saver, 97
rainy-day ideas, 121
recipes (fall)
  All-Butter Piecrust, 106–7
  Dinner in a Pumpkin, 98–99
  Fancy Crust, 105
  Homemade Applesauce, 92–93
  Perfectly Perfect Apple Pie, 108–9
  Thanksgiving Casserole, 116–17
recipes (spring)
  Carrot Cake, 38–39
  Chocolate Chip Oatmeal Banana Bars, 46–47
  Dog Treats, 26–27
  No-Bake Energy Balls, 32–33
  Popsicle Stick Numbers, 45
  Tater Tot Casserole, 18–19
recipes (summer)
  about: S'mores Station, 81
  Caramel Corn Snack, 58–59
  Homemade(ish) Dr. Cake, 66–67
  S'mores S'mores, 82–83
recipes (winter)
  Best Ever Sugar Cookies, 148–49
  Celebration Chocolate Chip Cookies, 154–55
  Gingie Cookie Kids & Easiest Royal Icing Ever, 132–33
  Grinch Cookies, 140–41

Sidewalk Popsicle Chalk, 40–44
silhouette, pet, 20–24
Silver Storage, 153
s'mores, 81, 82–83
snowman, hot cocoa, 136–38
sugar cookies, 148–49
Sunflower Wreath, 76–80 (156)

Tater Tot Casserole, 18–19
Thanksgiving Casserole, 116–17

umbrella, embellished, 14–16

Vacation Travel, 57

wreath, sunflower, 76–80 (156)